HOW TO FULFILL GOD'S WILL

PART 3 OF 3

How to Fulfill God's Will
ISBN: 978-1-59548-162-7

TABLE OF CONTENTS

HOW TO USE YOUR STUDY GUIDE

LESSON 11 • IN IT TO WIN IT   2

    LESSON 11.1   3
    OUTLINE 11.1   7
    TEACHER'S GUIDE 11.1   9
    DISCIPLESHIP QUESTIONS 11.1   12
    ANSWER KEY 11.1   15
    SCRIPTURES 11.1   16

    LESSON 11.2   17
    OUTLINE 11.2   22
    TEACHER'S GUIDE 11.2   24
    DISCIPLESHIP QUESTIONS 11.2   27
    ANSWER KEY 11.2   29
    SCRIPTURES 11.2   30

    LESSON 11.3   33
    OUTLINE 11.3   38
    TEACHER'S GUIDE 11.3   40
    DISCIPLESHIP QUESTIONS 11.3   42
    ANSWER KEY 11.3   44
    SCRIPTURES 11.3   45

LESSON 12 • PATIENT ENDURANCE   48

    LESSON 12.1   49
    OUTLINE 12.1   55
    TEACHER'S GUIDE 12.1   58
    DISCIPLESHIP QUESTIONS 12.1   62
    ANSWER KEY 12.1   65
    SCRIPTURES 12.1   66

    LESSON 12.2   69
    OUTLINE 12.2   75
    TEACHER'S GUIDE 12.2   77
    DISCIPLESHIP QUESTIONS 12.2   79
    ANSWER KEY 12.2   81
    SCRIPTURES 12.2   82

LESSON 13 • GLORIFY THE LORD   88

    LESSON 13.1   89
    OUTLINE 13.1   96
    TEACHER'S GUIDE 13.1   98
    DISCIPLESHIP QUESTIONS 13.1   101
    ANSWER KEY 13.1   104
    SCRIPTURES 13.1   105

    LESSON 13.2   109
    OUTLINE 13.2   115
    TEACHER'S GUIDE 13.2   117
    DISCIPLESHIP QUESTIONS 13.2   119
    ANSWER KEY 13.2   121
    SCRIPTURES 13.2   122

LESSON 14 • THANKFULNESS WILL TAKE YOU PLACES 124

 LESSON 14.1 125
 OUTLINE 14.1 131
 TEACHER'S GUIDE 14.1 132
 DISCIPLESHIP QUESTIONS 14.1 134
 ANSWER KEY 14.1 135
 SCRIPTURES 14.1 136

 LESSON 14.2 139
 OUTLINE 14.2 144
 TEACHER'S GUIDE 14.2 146
 DISCIPLESHIP QUESTIONS 14.2 149
 ANSWER KEY 14.2 151
 SCRIPTURES 14.2 152

LESSON 15 • PUTTING YOUR IMAGINATION TO WORK 154

 LESSON 15.1 155
 OUTLINE 15.1 159
 TEACHER'S GUIDE 15.1 160
 DISCIPLESHIP QUESTIONS 15.1 162
 ANSWER KEY 15.1 163
 SCRIPTURES 15.1 164

 LESSON 15.2 165
 OUTLINE 15.2 170
 TEACHER'S GUIDE 15.2 172
 DISCIPLESHIP QUESTIONS 15.2 174
 ANSWER KEY 15.2 176
 SCRIPTURES 15.2 177

 LESSON 15.3 179
 OUTLINE 15.3 185
 TEACHER'S GUIDE 15.3 187
 DISCIPLESHIP QUESTIONS 15.3 190
 ANSWER KEY 15.3 193
 SCRIPTURES 15.3 194

 LESSON 15.4 195
 OUTLINE 15.4 198
 TEACHER'S GUIDE 15.4 200
 DISCIPLESHIP QUESTIONS 15.4 202
 ANSWER KEY 15.4 203
 SCRIPTURES 15.4 204

ANDREW'S TEACHING RECOMMENDATIONS IN THIS STUDY GUIDE 205

OTHER RECOMMEDED TEACHINGS 206

HOW TO USE YOUR STUDY GUIDE

Whether you are teaching a class, leading a small group, discipling an individual, or studying on your own, this study guide is designed for you! Here's how it works:

Each study consists of a **Lesson**, **Outline**, **Teacher's Guide**, **Discipleship Questions**, **Answer Key**, and **Scriptures**—all of which have been divided into sections. Within the study, each section is a continuation of the previous section.

Outline for Group Study:
I. If possible, briefly review the previous study by going over the **Answer Key/Teacher's Guide** answers for the **Discipleship Questions/Teacher's Guide** questions.
II. Read the current section for the **Lesson** or **Teacher's Guide** aloud (e.g., 1.1, 1.2).
  A. Be sure that each student has a copy of the **Outline**.
  B. While the **Lesson** section or **Teacher's Guide** section is being read, students should use their **Outlines** to follow along.
III. Once the **Lesson** section or **Teacher's Guide** section is read, facilitate discussion and study using the **Discipleship Questions/Teacher's Guide** questions (the questions are all the same).
  A. Read aloud one question at a time.
  B. The group should use their **Outlines** to assist them in answering the questions.
  C. Have them read aloud each specifically mentioned scripture before answering the question.
  D. Discuss the answer/point from the **Lesson**, as desired.
  E. As much as possible, keep the discussion centered on the scriptures and the **Lesson** section or **Teacher's Guide** section points at hand.
  F. Remember, the goal is understanding (Matt. 13:19).
  G. One individual should not dominate the discussion, but try to draw out the quieter ones for the group conversation.
  H. Repeat the process until all of the questions are discussed/answered.

Materials Needed:
  Study guide, Bible, and enough copies of the **Outline**, **Discipleship Questions**, and **Scriptures** for each student. (Printable files of the **Outline**, **Discipleship Questions**, and **Scriptures** can be found on the CD-ROM included with this book.)

Outline for Personal Study:
I. Read the current **Lesson** section or **Teacher's Guide** section.
  A. Read additional information, if provided.
  B. Meditate on the given scriptures, as desired.
II. Answer the corresponding **Discipleship Questions/Teacher's Guide** questions.
III. Check your work with the **Answer Key/Teacher's Guide** answers.

Materials Needed:
  Study guide, Bible, and a writing utensil.

IN IT TO WIN IT

LESSON 11.1

It's one thing to find God's will and start moving in the right direction, but it's another to stay with it over the long haul. Anybody can start, but it's the people who stick with it and finish who really make a difference. We have all seen people who rise to popularity and influence like a shooting star and then burn out just as quickly. A lot of people seem to burn out almost from the start. Unfortunately, the body of Christ is cluttered with people who have fallen by the wayside.

I was part of the Charismatic movement during the 1970s, when millions of people were touched by the power of God in a significant way. But not all of those people are still seeking God today. I've heard a statistic that said that up to 70 percent of Charismatics no longer attend church. Our churches wouldn't have enough seats for everyone if they did!

The fact that you are reading a study guide about God's will is an indication that you are serious about your relationship with Him. You aren't just going to church on Sunday to pay a debt or do your duty. You are excited and seeking the things of God. I applaud you for your efforts; you are off to a great start. But not every person who gets off to a good start is going to finish his or her race. I'm not trying to be negative. I just want you to recognize the importance of learning how to fulfill God's will in your life, once you find it and begin to follow it.

Fortunately, I have some tips to help you stay on track. God doesn't determine that His power in your life will cease after a certain length of time, and then you will have to get a fresh touch from Him again—as if His power comes with an expiration date. No, it's totally up to you whether or not you stay full of God and excited about His plans for your life. I think this is good news because it means that if you aren't keyed up about following God, you can do something to get excited about the things of God.

Obedience

My teaching focuses on the grace of God. I try to get people free from the misconception of earning God's love or thinking that God will only move in their lives when they do everything right. God has never had anyone qualified working for Him yet—none of us deserve His love. We just have to humble ourselves and receive His love as a gift. Our ministry's focus on God's grace is one reason, I believe, that God has raised us up. Grace just isn't being emphasized enough in the body of Christ. Many people don't understand the simple truth that God isn't mad at them.

The grace of God is the Gospel message, but it sometimes causes a pendulum effect in people. In my estimation, the body of Christ is way out of balance on the side of legalism— trying to be holy and earn God's approval. Sometimes when people hear the Good News of God's grace and realize salvation doesn't depend upon living a holy life, they swing clear over to the other extreme of thinking that it doesn't matter what they do.

I'm not necessarily talking about living in sin, but sometimes people who were caught up in legalism quit seeking the Lord with all of their hearts, because they think everything is up to God. They don't recognize the balance between grace and faith.[1] Obedience may be a dirty word to some, but we have to learn to obey God if we want to finish our race and cross the finish line as winners. Obedience is inseparable from fulfilling God's will in our lives.

> *Come now, and let us reason together, saith the LORD: though your sins be as scarlet, they shall be as white as snow; though they be red like crimson, they shall be as wool. [19] If ye be willing and obedient, ye shall eat the good of the land.*
> ISAIAH 1:18-19

No one's sins have ever changed from crimson to white as snow through their own goodness. This only happens by grace. We have a Savior who paid for our sin, and that is the only way sin gets dealt with. Isaiah 1:19 says that we have to be willing and obedient in order to eat the good of the land. God deals with us based on His grace, but we have to obey what He tells us to do if we are going to finish our race and accomplish His plans.

Don't get me wrong; disobeying God doesn't change His grace nature. God still loves you. He isn't going to be upset with you—He accepts you through Jesus. Many people preach that if you don't obey God, you won't prosper. This leaves the impression that God is going to snub you or put you on the shelf because you didn't do what He told you to. They also say, "God won't use a dirty vessel." *I want you to know that God doesn't have any other kind of vessel to use!* You can't do everything right. God's purpose for you is completely separate from what you deserve.

Won't vs. Can't

Obeying God in order to experience all the blessings He desires to give us is not the same as saying God won't use us *unless* we obey Him. It isn't that God won't so much as He *can't*. If we don't follow God's leading, Satan is going to take advantage of our disobedience. Then the Enemy will come into our lives to steal, kill, and destroy.

> *Know ye not, that to whom ye yield yourselves servants to obey, his servants ye are to whom ye obey; whether of sin unto death, or of obedience unto righteousness?*
> ROMANS 6:16

Whomever we obey and make the master of our lives is going to control us. God calls us, but in order to fulfill our purpose, we have to follow His leading. If I was God, I wouldn't have picked me to do what I'm doing. It's not like I have everything going for me. God chose me in spite of who I am—that's grace. But if I hadn't obeyed Him and followed His leading, I wouldn't be where I am today. I wouldn't be seeing people's lives changed, and our ministry wouldn't be successful. I had to take steps to obey the Lord. God's love for me remains the same whether I obey Him or not, but the potential for His love to work through me to transform others depends upon me yielding to His leadership.

I can't tell you how many people over the years have told me that they were sure God told them to do some particular thing. But they had a thousand reasons they couldn't do it. They told me about their own natural limitations. They told me they didn't have enough money. They told me how this, that, and the other thing that happened.

I actually had a lady tell me she knew God was calling her to go to Charis Bible College, but she said, "I have two dogs. What would I do? How could I come to Bible school if I have two dogs?" I told her, "Just shoot 'em." Of course, I didn't really want her to shoot her dogs. I was just trying to help her see what is truly important. It's amazing the little things we let stand in the way. We say, "Well, I have a goldfish and a hangnail. I couldn't possibly do what You are asking me to do, Lord."

You are never going to fulfill God's calling on your life waiting around for every possible circumstance to line up perfectly. Jamie and I haven't done everything right the first time, but we have been quick to obey. We have stepped out when God called us to. We have done a few things in ways that I wouldn't necessarily recommend and we have made some mistakes along the way, but we have always tried to obey God, even when it looked like following Him wasn't in our best interest. In order to fulfill our purpose, we have to be willing to obey God no matter what.

This is so simple, yet so many people who know what God is calling them to do won't step out, because they are afraid of the cost. You can't fulfill God's will if you are afraid to step out and pursue it. Following God is going to cost you something. I can guarantee you that not everyone is going to support your decision. Proverbs says, *"The fear of man bringeth a snare: but whoso putteth his trust in the LORD shall be safe"* (Prov. 29:25). If you need to have people's approval before you step out on what God calls you to do, you are never going to make it.

Andrew's Recommendations for Further Study:

[1] This is a topic that deserves more attention than I can give it here. I have written a book called *Living in the Balance of Grace and Faith* that goes into far more detail. Also, you can access the free audio teaching for *Living in the Balance of Grace and Faith* on the AWM website: **www.awmi.net/extra/audio/1064**.

OUTLINE • 11.1

I. Anybody can start, but it's the people who stick with it and finish who really make a difference.

    A. Unfortunately, the body of Christ is cluttered with people who have fallen by the wayside.

    B. The fact that you are reading a study guide about God's will is an indication that you are serious about your relationship with Him—you are excited and seeking the things of God.

    C. But not every person who gets off to a good start is going to finish his or her race.

    D. I'm not trying to be negative—I just want you to recognize the importance of learning how to fulfill God's will in your life, once you find it and begin to follow it.

    E. It's totally up to you whether or not you stay full of God and excited about His plans for your life.

II. Obedience may be a dirty word to some, but we have to learn to obey God if we want to finish our race and cross the finish line as winners.

    A. Obedience is inseparable from fulfilling God's will in our lives.

    Come now, and let us reason together, saith the LORD: though your sins be as scarlet, they shall be as white as snow; though they be red like crimson, they shall be as wool. [19] If ye be willing and obedient, ye shall eat the good of the land.
    ISAIAH 1:18-19

    B. We have a Savior who paid for our sin, and that is the only way sin gets dealt with.

    C. Isaiah 1:19 says that we have to be willing and obedient in order to eat the good of the land.

    D. Disobeying God doesn't change His grace nature.

    E. God still loves us, and He isn't going to be upset with us—He accepts us through Jesus.

    F. God's purpose for us is completely separate from what we deserve.

III. Obeying God in order to experience all the blessings He desires to give us is not the same as saying God won't use us *unless* we obey Him.

    A. It isn't that God won't so much as He *can't*.

B. If we don't follow God's leading, Satan is going to take advantage of our disobedience.

Know ye not, that to whom ye yield yourselves servants to obey, his servants ye are to whom ye obey; whether of sin unto death, or of obedience unto righteousness?
ROMANS 6:16

C. Whomever we obey and make the master of our lives is going to control us.

D. God calls us, but in order to fulfill our purpose, we have to follow His leading.

E. We are never going to fulfill God's calling on our lives waiting around for every possible circumstance to line up perfectly.

F. This is so simple, yet so many people who know what God is calling them to do won't step out, because they are afraid of the cost.

G. I can guarantee that not everyone is going to support our decisions.

The fear of man bringeth a snare: but whoso putteth his trust in the Lord shall be safe.
PROVERBS 29:25

H. If we need to have people's approval before we step out on what God calls us to do, we are never going to make it.

Andrew's Recommendations for Further Study:

¹ This is a topic that deserves more attention than I can give it here. I have written a book called *Living in the Balance of Grace and Faith* that goes into far more detail. Also, you can access the free audio teaching for *Living in the Balance of Grace and Faith* on the AWM website: **www.awmi.net/extra/audio/1064**.

1. Anybody can start, but it's the people who stick with it and finish who really make a difference. Unfortunately, the body of Christ is cluttered with people who have fallen by the wayside. The fact that you are reading a study guide about God's will is an indication that you are serious about your relationship with Him—you are excited and seeking the things of God. But not every person who gets off to a good start is going to finish his or her race. I'm not trying to be negative—I just want you to recognize the importance of learning how to fulfill God's will in your life, once you find it and begin to follow it. It's totally up to you whether or not you stay full of God and excited about His plans for your life.

1a.   Anybody can start, but who really makes a difference?
<u>The people who stick with it and finish</u>

1b.   Discussion question: How does knowing God's will for your life help you finish your race?
<u>Discussion question</u>

1c.   It's totally up to _____ whether or not you stay full of God and excited about His plans for your life.
      A. God
      B. Your pastor
      C. Andrew
      D. Fate
      E. You
      <u>E. You</u>

2. Obedience may be a dirty word to some, but we have to learn to obey God if we want to finish our race and cross the finish line as winners. Obedience is inseparable from fulfilling God's will in our lives.

> *Come now, and let us reason together, saith the Lord: though your sins be as scarlet, they shall be as white as snow; though they be red like crimson, they shall be as wool. [19] If ye be willing and obedient, ye shall eat the good of the land.*
>
> ISAIAH 1:18-19

We have a Savior who paid for our sin, and that is the only way sin gets dealt with. Isaiah 1:19 says that we have to be willing and obedient in order to eat the good of the land. Disobeying God doesn't change His grace nature. God still loves us, and He isn't going to be upset with us—He accepts us through Jesus. God's purpose for us is completely separate from what we deserve.

2a.   Discussion question: What are some examples—from Scripture and/or from your own life—of people who have been obedient to God? Share what you can learn from these people and their actions.
Discussion question

2b.   Obedience is inseparable from what?
Fulfilling God's will in your life

2c.   Isaiah 1:18 says, *"Come now, and let us reason together, saith the Lord: though your sins be as scarlet, they shall be as _____ as snow; though they be red like _____, they shall be as wool."*
"White" / "crimson"

2d.   According to Isaiah 1:19, what will happen if you are willing and obedient?
You will eat the good of the land

2e.   Discussion question: Does your thinking line up with the Word when it comes to God's attitude toward you; i.e., that God loves you, He isn't upset with you, He accepts you through Jesus, etc.? If not, what are some areas where you might need to renew your mind?
Discussion question

3. Obeying God in order to experience all the blessings He desires to give us is not the same as saying that God won't use us *unless* we obey Him. It isn't that God won't so much as He *can't*. If we don't follow God's leading, Satan is going to take advantage of our disobedience (Rom. 6:16). Whomever we obey and make the master of our lives is going to control us. God calls us, but in order to fulfill our purpose, we have to follow His leading. We are never going to fulfill God's calling on our lives waiting around for every possible circumstance to line up perfectly. This is so simple, yet so many people who know what God is calling them to do won't step out, because they are afraid of the cost. I can guarantee that not everyone is going to support our decisions. If we need to have people's approval before we step out on what God calls us to do, we are never going to make it (Prov. 29:25).

3a.   Discussion question: What is the difference between the idea of obeying God in order to experience all His blessings and the idea that God won't use you *unless* you obey Him?
Discussion question

3b.   *"Know ye not, that to whom ye _____ yourselves servants to obey, his servants ye are to whom ye obey; whether of sin unto _____, or of obedience unto _____?"* (Rom. 6:16).
"Yield" / "death" / "righteousness"

3c.   You are never going to fulfill God's calling on your life by doing what?
Waiting around for every possible circumstance to line up perfectly

3d.   Discussion question: In what ways, if any, has fear kept you from stepping out and doing what God has called you to do?
Discussion question

3e.   What does Proverbs 29:25 say?
"The fear of man bringeth a snare: but whoso putteth his trust in the LORD shall be safe"

DISCIPLESHIP QUESTIONS • 11.1

1. Anybody can start, but who really makes a difference?

_____

_____

_____

2. Discussion question: How does knowing God's will for your life help you finish your race?

_____

_____

_____

3. It's totally up to _____ whether or not you stay full of God and excited about His plans for your life.
   A. God
   B. Your pastor
   C. Andrew
   D. Fate
   E. You

4. Discussion question: What are some examples—from Scripture and/or from your own life—of people who have been obedient to God. Share what you can learn from these people and their actions.

_____

_____

_____

5. Obedience is inseparable from what?

_____

_____

_____

6. Isaiah 1:18 says, _"Come now, and let us reason together, saith the LORD: though your sins be as scarlet, they shall be as _____ as snow; though they be red like _____, they shall be as wool."_

7. According to Isaiah 1:19, what will happen if you are willing and obedient?

_____

_____

_____

8. Discussion question: Does your thinking line up with the Word when it comes to God's attitude toward you; i.e., that God loves you, He isn't upset with you, He accepts you through Jesus, etc.? If not, what are some areas where you might need to renew your mind?

_____

_____

_____

9. Discussion question: What is the difference between the idea of obeying God in order to experience all His blessings and the idea that God won't use you *unless* you obey Him?

_____

_____

_____

10. *"Know ye not, that to whom ye _____ yourselves servants to obey, his servants ye are to whom ye obey; whether of sin unto _____, or of obedience unto _____?"* (Rom. 6:16).

11. You are never going to fulfill God's calling on your life by doing what?

_____

_____

_____

12. Discussion question: In what ways, if any, has fear kept you from stepping out and doing what God has called you to do?

_____

_____

_____

13. What does Proverbs 29:25 say?

_____

_____

_____

ANSWER KEY • 11.1

1. The people who stick with it and finish
2. *Discussion question*
3. E. You
4. *Discussion question*
5. Fulfilling God's will in your life
6. *"White" / "crimson"*
7. You will eat the good of the land
8. *Discussion question*
9. *Discussion question*
10. *"Yield" / "death" / "righteousness"*
11. Waiting around for every possible circumstance to line up perfectly
12. *Discussion question*
13. *"The fear of man bringeth a snare: but whoso putteth his trust in the LORD shall be safe"*

ISAIAH 1:18-19

Come now, and let us reason together, saith the LORD: though your sins be as scarlet, they shall be as white as snow; though they be red like crimson, they shall be as wool. [19] If ye be willing and obedient, ye shall eat the good of the land.

ROMANS 6:16

Know ye not, that to whom ye yield yourselves servants to obey, his servants ye are to whom ye obey; whether of sin unto death, or of obedience unto righteousness?

PROVERBS 29:25

The fear of man bringeth a snare: but whoso putteth his trust in the Lord shall be safe.

LESSON 11.2

But be ye doers of the word, and not hearers only, deceiving your own selves. [23] For if any be a hearer of the word, and not a doer, he is like unto a man beholding his natural face in a glass: [24] For he beholdeth himself, and goeth his way, and straightway forgetteth what manner of man he was. [25] But whoso looketh into the perfect law of liberty, and continueth therein, he being not a forgetful hearer, but a doer of the work, this man shall be blessed in his deed.

JAMES 1:22-25

It isn't enough just to hear God's voice; you have to *do* what He says in order to fulfill your purpose in life. God isn't going to give you step number two or step number ten if you haven't obeyed step number one. You move into God's will for your life by stages: the good, the acceptable, and the perfect (Rom. 12:2). God's will is always perfect, but the degree to which you experience His perfect will changes relative to how much you cooperate with His plans. God shows you things step by step—which means you have to act on what He leads you to do before you will ever see the next step.

Hearing and obeying God—or failing to obey—causes a ripple effect in our lives. We know, for instance, that we should give money to support the preaching of the Gospel. The Bible teaches us to honor the Lord with our substance and with the first fruits of our increase (Prov. 3:9). People know this, but they don't obey. Then they wonder why other things in their lives aren't working. Jesus said if we aren't faithful in that which is least, we won't be faithful over much (Luke 16:10). In context, Jesus was saying that money is the least area we can trust God for. Trusting God with our finances is the *smallest* use of our faith. If we don't trust God with our money, we won't trust Him in other areas either.

A lot of people say they trust God for their salvation, but they grasp at their money like they don't trust Him to provide for their physical needs. How can you trust God with your eternal redemption, but not trust Him for *"that which is least"*? If you can't do the least, you can't do the greatest. You can't lift 200 pounds if you're not able to lift 20. Likewise, you can't do great things for God unless you can trust Him with your finances.

Every one of the mature Christians I know is a giver—without exception. They all trust God. You can't become a mature believer without trusting God in your finances. Conversely, I know a lot of Christians who look good on the outside, but I'm not sure if they are still going to be following God the next time I see them. Those are the people who don't trust God in their giving. Giving is an indicator of where you put your trust.

Trusting God in the area of your finances isn't just for "super-saints." Trusting God is basic to your faith. Some people know what the Word of God says about finances, but they aren't doing it. Then they wonder why they aren't prospering or being healed in their bodies. It isn't because God won't heal you until you trust Him; it's because your lack of trust undermines your faith and prevents you from receiving the healing that God has already provided for you.

In terms of trusting God, you have to start where you are. You have to be able to lift five pounds before you can lift a hundred. If you can't trust God in the area of your finances, Satan will stop your physical healing by using the fear you are embracing. It isn't that God won't bless you; it's that Satan is stealing from you because you haven't obeyed God.

Whomever you yield yourself to as a servant will rule over you—whether you obey sin and fear, which leads to death, or serve obedience to righteousness and the Word of God, which leads to life. Yielding to fear, greed, or selfishness in your life is the same as yielding to Satan—who is the author of those things. Yielding to Satan allows him to hinder you from receiving from God. It can stop your healing, it can stop your marriage from working, it can stop any number of things—because you aren't trusting God.

On the other hand, trusting God empowers Him to move in your life. Blinders fall from your eyes, and you begin to get revelation from the Word like never before. You will start experiencing God's supernatural supply for your needs, causing you to trust Him even more. Fear empowers the Enemy; faith empowers God.

Obeying God is important. Giving money to support the Gospel is just one example of how obeying, or failing to obey, affects other areas of your life. The same is true in the area of husbands loving their wives, wives respecting their husbands, assembling together with other believers, and on and on it could go. Failing to obey God in areas where He has already given you direction gives Satan an inroad into your life.

Satan did not originally have authority to oppress the earth. God gave dominion over the earth to Adam and Eve (Gen. 1:26-28). They turned over their authority to Satan when they were tempted and gave in to him. We empower the devil by our actions in exactly the same way. Satan is powerless on his own. He needs physical human beings to yield to him and empower him.

Actions are linked to obedience. We release the power of God by acting on what He has told us to do. We release the power of the devil through our wrong actions, or lack of action. When God tells us to do something and we don't do it, we yield ourselves to Satan—the author of the fear or temptation that is keeping us from obeying God. When we yield to Satan, it empowers him to wreak havoc in our lives.

Sexual purity is an area that seems to trip a lot of people up. I've heard about unmarried couples who are living together while trying to use God's grace as an excuse for living in sin. It's true that God loves them; He's not mad at them, and He isn't going to punish them. God loves us whether we are married and living godly lives or not. It may offend some people to hear that, but it's true.

Jesus ministered to a woman living under the same circumstances. He showed her love and offered to give her living water (John 4:4-26). God isn't mad at you if you aren't married to the person you are shacking up with, but your disobedience is giving Satan an inroad into your life. The Lord didn't say that you are supposed to be united to one person in marriage because He is a spoilsport; He did it because He knows what is best for you. God knows how divorce and broken relationships hurt people. He also knows what makes you happy.

God created Adam and Eve, not Adam and Steve. God said that it's not good for a man to be alone, so he made a woman—not another man. God's plan is for us to live in heterosexual relationships. But He loves homosexuals too. The grace of God applies to everyone. He's not mad at people for living a gay lifestyle. God loves homosexuals, but living that way gives Satan a huge inroad into their lives.

Anyone who wants to fulfill God's will doesn't have the luxury of giving Satan access to their life. The Enemy is out to kill you. He is out to destroy your life and stop you from fulfilling God's will. Intentionally failing to do what God has directed you to do, through the Bible or otherwise, is like walking up to Satan and telling him to take his best shot. When Satan cleans your clock, don't go to God and ask Him why He let it happen. He didn't let it happen—*you* let it happen. You gave Satan free access. You gave him an inroad into your life. You can't live in sin and prosper. Sooner or later, it's going to catch up with you.

God doesn't turn away from us because of sin or imperfection. If He did, He would have turned away from the entire human race, because none of us are perfect (Rom. 3:23). God doesn't change the way He relates to us according to our behavior; His grace is always the same. But Satan is out to hinder us. We can't let him come into our lives and encumber us with all sorts of weight, and still win the race. It doesn't work that way. We need to obey God if we want to finish our race.

Saving Faith

What doth it profit, my brethren, though a man say he hath faith, and have not works? can faith save him? [17] ... faith, if it hath not works, is dead, being alone.
JAMES 2:14 AND 17

Scripture says that we are saved by grace through faith (Eph. 2:8), so faith does save. Yet James 2:14 and 17 is asking whether faith can save a man who doesn't have works. The point here is that faith is never alone. Saving faith is always accompanied by action. If someone runs into a crowded movie theater and shouts "Fire!"—there will be some accompanying action. Everyone who really believes there is a fire is going to act. Some people might faint, some might scream, others might panic or run, but everyone who believes that there's a fire is going to do something.

Anyone who says "I believe" but doesn't act on it doesn't really believe. If you really believe God is your source, then you will give from your resources. If you trust God, there will be evidence of it in your life. Your actions reveal what you truly believe. Faith alone saves, but saving faith is never alone—it causes action. Your actions are vital to your faith. James went on to say,

Yea, a man may say, Thou hast faith, and I have works: shew me thy faith without thy works, and I will shew thee my faith by my works. [19] Thou believest that there is one God; thou doest well: the devils also believe, and tremble.
JAMES 2:18-19

This is one of the most sarcastic statements in the entire Bible. You believe that there is one God? Good. But you haven't done anything the devil hasn't done. The devil believes, to the point that he trembles, but his actions don't correspond to faith. Satan knows that God exists, but his actions are against God.

But wilt thou know, O vain man, that faith without works is dead?
JAMES 2:20

The devil believes—but his works are against God; therefore, he doesn't have saving faith. People can say "Oh, I believe God exists," but if their actions are contrary to the Lord's direction, then they aren't believing with "saving faith." They only have mental assent. Faith without corresponding action is not true faith.

During the time that Jamie and I were struggling financially, I painted houses for a little while to make ends meet. One day I felt sick, so I went home during my lunch break. I was so sick, I couldn't even sit up. I was scheduled to get paid that day, so I needed to go back and finish work. But I only felt like lying down and taking a nap.

"You can't stay home today," Jamie said to me. "We need this money."

So, Jamie prayed for me to be healed. I still felt bad, though, so I started to lie back down on the couch. Jamie said, "Oh, no, you're not. You are *not* going to act sick."

She put her arm around me, stood me up, and walked me all through the house—dancing and jumping. At first, she was dancing, and I was being dragged around. I was praying for healing, but I wanted to act sick because that's how I felt. Jamie made me start acting like I was healed. By the end of my lunch break, I felt totally normal. I went back to work that afternoon and got paid. But I didn't feel well until I started *acting* well.

Faith doesn't reach completion until we begin to act in accordance with what we profess to believe—action must be joined together with belief. We can't just quit taking medicine, thinking the action of stopping our medicine is going to make us well. People die doing foolish things like that. The Bible says with the heart man believes, and with the mouth confession is made (Rom. 10:10). First we have to believe in our hearts that God has healed us; *then* we can act on what we believe. If we believe with our hearts and confess with our mouths, we will see it come to pass. *Actions follow faith—they don't generate faith.* Faith has to come first. We believe with our hearts, and our faith will be made perfect as we begin to act on what we believe.

IV. It isn't enough just to hear God's voice; you have to *do* what He says in order to fulfill your purpose in life.

*But be ye doers of the word, and not hearers only, deceiving your own selves.
[23] For if any be a hearer of the word, and not a doer, he is like unto a man
beholding his natural face in a glass: [24] For he beholdeth himself, and goeth his
way, and straightway forgetteth what manner of man he was. [25] But whoso
looketh into the perfect law of liberty, and continueth therein, he being not a
forgetful hearer, but a doer of the work, this man shall be blessed in his deed.*

JAMES 1:22-25

A. You move into God's will for your life by stages: the good, the acceptable, and the perfect (Rom. 12:2).

B. God's will is always perfect, but the degree to which you experience His perfect will changes relative to how much you cooperate with His plans.

C. God shows you things step by step—which means you have to act on what He leads you to do before you will ever see the next step.

D. Hearing and obeying God—or failing to obey—causes a ripple effect in your life.

E. For example, if you don't trust God with your money, you won't trust Him in other areas either.

F. Giving is an indicator of where you put your trust.

G. Trusting God in the area of your finances isn't just for "super-saints"—trusting God is basic to your faith.

H. Failing to obey God in areas where He has already given you direction gives Satan an inroad into your life.

I. You release the power of God by acting on what He has told you to do.

J. You release the power of the devil through your wrong actions, or lack of action.

K. When God tells you to do something and you don't do it, you yield yourself to Satan—the author of the fear or temptation that is keeping you from obeying God.

L. God doesn't change the way He relates to you according to your behavior; His grace is always the same.

M. But Satan is out to hinder you.

N. You can't let Satan come into your life and encumber you with all sorts of weight, and still win the race.

O. You need to obey God if you want to finish your race.

V.   Saving faith (Eph. 2:8) is always accompanied by action.

What doth it profit, my brethren, though a man say he hath faith, and have not works? can faith save him? [17] ... faith, if it hath not works, is dead, being alone.
JAMES 2:14 AND 17

A.   Anyone who says "I believe" but doesn't act on it doesn't really believe.

B.   Your actions reveal what you truly believe.

Yea, a man may say, Thou hast faith, and I have works: shew me thy faith without thy works, and I will shew thee my faith by my works. [19] Thou believest that there is one God; thou doest well: the devils also believe, and tremble. [20] But wilt thou know, O vain man, that faith without works is dead?
JAMES 2:18-20

C.   The devil believes—but his works are against God; therefore, he doesn't have saving faith.

D.   Faith without corresponding action is not true faith.

E.   The Bible says with the heart man believes, and with the mouth confession is made (Rom. 10:10).

F.   If you believe with your heart and confess with your mouth, you will see it come to pass.

G.   *Actions follow faith—they don't generate faith.*

H.   You believe with your heart, and your faith will be made perfect as you begin to act on what you believe.

4. It isn't enough just to hear God's voice; you have to *do* what He says in order to fulfill your purpose in life.

> *But be ye doers of the word, and not hearers only, deceiving your own selves.* *[23] For if any be a hearer of the word, and not a doer, he is like unto a man beholding his natural face in a glass: [24] For he beholdeth himself, and goeth his way, and straightway forgetteth what manner of man he was. [25] But whoso looketh into the perfect law of liberty, and continueth therein, he being not a forgetful hearer, but a doer of the work, this man shall be blessed in his deed.*
>
> JAMES 1:22-25

You move into God's will for your life by stages: the good, the acceptable, and the perfect (Rom. 12:2). God's will is always perfect, but the degree to which you experience His perfect will changes relative to how much you cooperate with His plans. God shows you things step by step—which means you have to act on what He leads you to do before you will ever see the next step. Hearing and obeying God—or failing to obey—causes a ripple effect in your life. For example, if you don't trust God with your money, you won't trust Him in other areas either. Giving is an indicator of where you put your trust. Trusting God in the area of your finances isn't just for "super-saints"—trusting God is basic to your faith. Failing to obey God in areas where He has already given you direction gives Satan an inroad into your life. You release the power of God by acting on what He has told you to do. You release the power of the devil through your wrong actions, or lack of action. When God tells you to do something and you don't do it, you yield yourself to Satan—the author of the fear or temptation that is keeping you from obeying God. God doesn't change the way He relates to you according to your behavior; His grace is always the same. But Satan is out to hinder you. You can't let Satan come into your life and encumber you with all sorts of weight, and still win the race. You need to obey God if you want to finish your race.

4a. James 1:22 says, *"But be ye _____ of the word, and not _____ only, deceiving your own selves."*
 "Doers" / "hearers"

4b. You move into God's will for your life by stages (Rom. 12:2). What are these stages?
 The good, the acceptable, and the perfect

4c. *Discussion question:* What is the step God has for you now? Has God shown you your next step yet? What do you believe that is?
 Discussion question

4d. Giving is an indicator of where you put your _____.
 A. Cash
 B. Hat
 C. Trust
 D. All of the above
 E. None of the above
 C. Trust

4e. How do you release the power of God?
By acting on what He has told you to do

4f. How do you release the power of the devil?
Through your wrong actions, or lack of action

5. Saving faith (Eph. 2:8) is always accompanied by action.

> *What doth it profit, my brethren, though a man say he hath faith, and have not works? can faith save him? [17] Even so faith, if it hath not works, is dead, being alone.*
>
> JAMES 2:14 AND 17

Anyone who says "I believe" but doesn't act on it, doesn't really believe. Your actions reveal what you truly believe.

> *Yea, a man may say, Thou hast faith, and I have works: shew me thy faith without thy works, and I will shew thee my faith by my works. [19] Thou believest that there is one God; thou doest well: the devils also believe, and tremble. [20] But wilt thou know, O vain man, that faith without works is dead?*
>
> JAMES 2:18-20

The devil believes—but his works are against God; therefore, he doesn't have saving faith. Faith without corresponding action is not true faith. The Bible says with the heart man believes and with the mouth confession is made (Rom. 10:10). If you believe with your heart and confess with your mouth, you will see it come to pass. *Actions follow faith—they don't generate faith.* You believe with your heart, and your faith will be made perfect as you begin to act on what you believe.

5a. Discussion question: What do James 2:14 and 17 mean to you?
Discussion question

5b. According to James 2:18-20, the devil believes in God, so why isn't he saved?
His works are against God; therefore, he doesn't have saving faith

5c. True or False: The Bible says that with the head, man believes, and with the mouth, confession is made (Rom. 10:10).
False

5d. Actions _____ faith—they don't _____ faith.
Follow / generate

14. James 1:22 says, *"But be ye _____ of the word, and not _____ only, deceiving your own selves."*

15. You move into God's will for your life by stages (Rom. 12:2). What are these stages?

_____

_____

_____

16. Discussion question: What is the step God has for you now? Has God shown you your next step yet? What do you believe that is?

_____

_____

_____

17. Giving is an indicator of where you put your _____.
    A. Cash
    B. Hat
    C. Trust
    D. All of the above
    E. None of the above

18. How do you release the power of God?

_____

_____

_____

19. How do you release the power of the devil?

_____

_____

_____

20. Discussion question: What do James 2:14 and 17 mean to you?

_____

_____

_____

21. According to James 2:18-20, the devil believes in God, so why isn't he saved?

_____

_____

_____

22. True or False: The Bible says that with the head, man believes, and with the mouth, confession is made (Rom. 10:10).

23. Actions _____ faith—they don't _____ faith.

ANSWER KEY • 11.2

14. *"Doers" / "hearers"*
15. The good, the acceptable, and the perfect
16. *Discussion question*
17. C. Trust
18. By acting on what He has told you to do
19. Through your wrong actions, or lack of action
20. *Discussion question*
21. His works are against God; therefore, he doesn't have saving faith
22. False
23. Follow / generate

JAMES 1:22-25

But be ye doers of the word, and not hearers only, deceiving your own selves. [23] For if any be a hearer of the word, and not a doer, he is like unto a man beholding his natural face in a glass: [24] For he beholdeth himself, and goeth his way, and straightway forgetteth what manner of man he was. [25] But whoso looketh into the perfect law of liberty, and continueth therein, he being not a forgetful hearer, but a doer of the work, this man shall be blessed in his deed.

ROMANS 12:2

And be not conformed to this world: but be ye transformed by the renewing of your mind, that ye may prove what is that good, and acceptable, and perfect, will of God.

PROVERBS 3:9

Honour the LORD with thy substance, and with the firstfruits of all thine increase.

LUKE 16:10

He that is faithful in that which is least is faithful also in much: and he that is unjust in the least is unjust also in much.

GENESIS 1:26-28

And God said, Let us make man in our image, after our likeness: and let them have dominion over the fish of the sea, and over the fowl of the air, and over the cattle, and over all the earth, and over every creeping thing that creepeth upon the earth. [27] So God created man in his own image, in the image of God created he him; male and female created he them. [28] And God blessed them, and God said unto them, Be fruitful, and multiply, and replenish the earth, and subdue it: and have dominion over the fish of the sea, and over the fowl of the air, and over every living thing that moveth upon the earth.

JOHN 4:4-26

And he must needs go through Samaria. [5] Then cometh he to a city of Samaria, which is called Sychar, near to the parcel of ground that Jacob gave to his son Joseph. [6] Now Jacob's well was there. Jesus therefore, being wearied with his journey, sat thus on the well: and it was about the sixth hour. [7] There cometh a woman of Samaria to draw water: Jesus saith unto her, Give me to drink. [8] (For his disciples were gone away unto the city to buy meat.) [9] Then saith the woman of Samaria unto him, How is it that thou, being a Jew, askest drink of me, which am a woman of Samaria? for the Jews have no dealings with the Samaritans. [10] Jesus answered and said unto her, If thou knewest the gift of God, and who it is that saith to thee, Give me to drink; thou wouldest have asked of him, and he would have given thee living water. [11] The woman saith unto him, Sir, thou hast nothing to draw with, and the well is deep: from whence then hast thou that living water? [12] Art thou greater than our father Jacob, which gave us the well, and drank thereof himself, and his children, and his cattle? [13] Jesus answered and said unto her, Whosoever drinketh of this water shall thirst again: [14] But whosoever drinketh of the water that I shall give him shall never thirst; but the water that I shall give him shall be in him a well of water springing up into everlasting life. [15] The woman saith unto him, Sir, give me this water, that I thirst not, neither come hither to draw. [16] Jesus saith unto her, Go, call thy husband, and come hither. [17] The woman answered and said, I have no husband. Jesus said unto her, Thou hast well said, I have no husband: [18] For thou hast had five husbands; and he whom thou now hast is not thy husband: in that saidst thou truly. [19] The woman saith unto him, Sir, I perceive that thou art a prophet. [20] Our fathers worshipped in this mountain; and ye say, that in Jerusalem is the place where men ought to worship. [21] Jesus saith unto her, Woman, believe me, the hour cometh, when ye shall neither in this mountain, nor yet at Jerusalem, worship the Father. [22] Ye worship ye know not what: we know what we worship: for salvation is of the Jews. [23] But the hour cometh, and now is, when the true worshippers shall worship the Father in spirit and in truth: for the Father seeketh such to worship him. [24] God is a Spirit: and they that worship him must worship him in spirit and in truth. [25] The woman saith unto him, I know that Messias cometh, which is called Christ: when he is come, he will tell us all things. [26] Jesus saith unto her, I that speak unto thee am he.

ROMANS 3:23

For all have sinned, and come short of the glory of God.

JAMES 2:14

What doth it profit, my brethren, though a man say he hath faith, and have not works? can faith save him?

JAMES 2:17-20

Even so faith, if it hath not works, is dead, being alone. **[18]** Yea, a man may say, Thou hast faith, and I have works: shew me thy faith without thy works, and I will shew thee my faith by my works. **[19]** Thou believest that there is one God; thou doest well: the devils also believe, and tremble. **[20]** But wilt thou know, O vain man, that faith without works is dead?

EPHESIANS 2:8

For by grace are ye saved through faith; and that not of yourselves: it is the gift of God.

ROMANS 10:10

For with the heart man believeth unto righteousness; and with the mouth confession is made unto salvation.

LESSON 11.3

Many Christians are more dominated by their emotions than by what they believe. They let their feelings control how they act instead of letting faith steer them. Seeing God's will fulfilled in your life means learning to obey Him no matter how you feel. After you have heard God's direction and learned how to follow His will, you have to learn to be obedient to see His will fulfilled in your life. I highly recommend that you obey God in every area of your life—even if you feel like you simply can't do what God is leading you to do. Trust God and follow His leading. He will never lead you to do something you can't do or something that isn't in your best interest.

You can always do what God is asking you to do. You may lack the motivation, but you *can* do it if you really want to. Several years ago, my nephew came to me after he had received two or three speeding tickets and was about to have his license revoked.

"I can't help it," he said. "I just drive fast."

"That's not true," I told him. "You can help it."

"No, honest, I can't," he replied.

"If I was to sit in the backseat of your car with a gun pointed at your head and threatened to pull the trigger the moment you go over fifty-five miles an hour, could you drive less than fifty-five?" I asked.

"Well, yeah, I guess," he said.

"See," I said, "you can do it. You just lack the motivation."

Modern society tends to avoid responsibility at all costs. Our culture is always trying to shift the blame onto someone else or some exterior circumstance—anything other than accepting responsibility ourselves. People have a tendency to excuse all kinds of behavior because no one wants to be responsible for their actions. The real culprit, we're told, is the dysfunctional household we were raised in, our hormones, or because we are middle-aged or a teenager. The truth is, there are always reasons we are the way we are, but there are no excuses.

To fulfill God's will, you have to accept responsibility in your life. You aren't an evolved animal simply responding to stimuli. You are a person created in the image of God; therefore, you are responsible for your actions. Quit blaming other people for your current situation. Maybe some terrible things happened to you in the past, but you can accept responsibility for any wrong choices you have made in response and move on with your life. As long as you play the role of a victim, you will never be a victor.

God commanded believers: *"Rejoice in the Lord alway: and again I say, Rejoice"* (Phil. 4:4). I believe the reason He said *"and* again *I say, Rejoice"* (emphasis mine) is because He knew people were going to think, *He couldn't possibly have meant* always. Regardless of what you are going through, God says you can rejoice. It doesn't matter if you're going through a divorce, someone close to you has died, or if some other tragedy has struck your life. God would be unjust to command you to *"rejoice in the Lord alway"* if it wasn't possible.

Jesus said, *"In the world ye shall have tribulation: but be of good cheer; I have overcome the world"* (John 16:33). He admitted that we are going to have problems, but He told us to be of good cheer. The word *"rejoice"* is a verb—it's an action, not something we possess. We don't have to feel joy to rejoice in the Lord, because we always have joy in our spirits, whether we can feel it or not (Gal. 5:22). We can rejoice through gritted teeth or with tears running down our faces.

We can do what God tells us to do regardless of how we feel. Once we start obeying God, we will discover that we have a well on the inside of us that is full of the life of God. Rejoicing is like putting a bucket down into the well of life in our spirits and drawing out the fullness of God. We may start rejoicing through gritted teeth, but if we keep rejoicing, we will draw out the life of God that's inside of us. We will experience real joy and peace. We can't be led through life by our emotions. We have to be led by the Spirit of God.

One thing that distinguishes an adult from a child is the fact that adults try not to base their decisions on how they feel. As adults, we don't always feel like going to work, but we do it because we know we need to. We don't always feel like being the parent; sometimes, we want to be the child and fall down on the floor, throw a fit, and shout, "I didn't ask for this!"

But as parents, we know we need to be responsible and act like it. Yet, when it comes to our emotions, we don't take control. Most of us let emotions dominate our lives and dictate our behavior. Emotions should be like the caboose on a train—going wherever the train goes—but not determining anything.

Sometimes I don't feel like praying for people. When I first started in ministry, I didn't think God was doing anything unless I had a tingling sensation shooting up and down my spine. Praise God, I had enough sense to keep my mouth shut. I simply kept praying over people and believing that as the Bible says, when Christians lay hands on the sick, they will recover. So, I just kept praying for people. Soon I discovered that I saw some of the greatest miracles when I felt absolutely nothing when I prayed. Those experiences helped me learn not to be led by my feelings.

A Place Called There

And Elijah the Tishbite, who was of the inhabitants of Gilead, said unto Ahab, As the LORD God of Israel liveth, before whom I stand, there shall not be dew nor rain these years, but according to my word.

1 KINGS 17:1

Elijah received a word from God and acted on it. You have to understand the historical background to fully appreciate this story. Ahab and his wife, Jezebel, had outlawed the worship of God and were killing all of God's prophets. Elijah was putting his life on the line to deliver a prophecy to Ahab. He could have focused on the dangers to himself, but instead, he was obedient to the Lord—he received a word from God and *acted* on it.

Ahab knew that Elijah had prophesied the drought, so when it came, he searched every nation and kingdom to find Elijah (1 Kin. 18:10). Three and a half years later, Elijah finally showed himself to Ahab and instructed him to gather all of the false prophets of Baal together in one place. The king obeyed—he was actually taking orders from Elijah!

Elijah became the most dominant man in the entire nation because he received direction from God and acted on it. If he had stayed in his prayer closet and prayed for a drought, without confronting Ahab, the king would never have obeyed him—and Elijah wouldn't have initiated the greatest revival Israel had ever seen.

Immediately after Elijah prophesied the drought, God gave him further direction:

Get thee hence, and turn thee eastward, and hide thyself by the brook Cherith, that is before Jordan. [4] And it shall be, that thou shalt drink of the brook; and I have commanded the ravens to feed thee there. [5] So he went and did according unto the word of the LORD.

1 KINGS 17:3-5A

God gave Elijah a promise of protection, but notice that the promise to provide for Elijah didn't come until *after* he obeyed God's first instruction. This is why so many people don't fulfill God's will for their lives. God reveals His will, but people start trying to rationalize how everything is going to work out before they act on what He has told them to do. God didn't make provision for Elijah until *after* he acted on the first thing He told him to do. I made this same point earlier: God won't show you steps two through ten until you obey step one.

After Elijah obeyed the first thing God told him to do, He said, "Now go to the brook Cherith; I have commanded the ravens to feed you *there.*" God sent Elijah's provision *there*— not where Elijah was but where God told him to go. Also, notice that God had already commanded the provision. This is similar to how a quarterback throws the football to the receiver: He doesn't throw the ball to where the receiver is when the ball is leaving his hand; he throws it where receiver is going to be when the ball gets there. He throws the ball out in *front* of the receiver.

Likewise, God doesn't send your provision to *you*; He sends your provision to where He told you to *go.* God might lead you to start a business or step out in faith and begin a new path. Wherever God might lead you, you won't see the provision where you are now; you will see it *there*—after you act on what He told you to do. You can't make following God's leading conditional upon seeing His provision first. God has already sent His provision; it's on the way to where He told you to go, or it's already waiting there for you. One reason you might not be seeing God's provision in your life is because you are too much *here* and not enough *there.*

When God provided the $3.2 million we needed to renovate our building, He told me not to take out a loan—to trust Him for another way. After I obligated myself to see the provision come through my ministry partners, God sent His provision. When I made the decision to build debt free, my accounting books indicated that it would take a hundred years to save that amount of money. However, after I acted on what God told me to do, He supplied the money in *fourteen months!*

Today our ministry has taken a $50 million step of faith. Some people might think it's crazy to do that; but God told us to go there, so we're going. Our provision is *there*, and the closer we get to where God is telling us to go, the more of His provision we will see. We are building a brand-new facility for Charis Bible College that will prepare thousands of believers to go out and make disciples of every nation. It's God's plan, so He will bring it to pass.

By acting on God's direction, Elijah saw the greatest revival that had ever happened until his time. He didn't know how God was going to protect and provide for him until *after* he obeyed the first word God gave him. Many born-again, Spirit-filled believers look at their lives and only see problems. They don't understand that they have the same power on the inside of them that raised Jesus Christ from the dead (Eph. 1:18-20). *God's power isn't out in heaven someplace—it's on the inside of us.*

Believers need to act on the instruction God has given them. For instance, the Bible says that speaking in tongues is rest and refreshing (Is. 28:11-12). So, if you are discouraged and need to be refreshed, speak in tongues. I guarantee it will get you fired up. Instead of looking for a "fresh" word from God to fix your problem, act on the direction He has already given you in Scripture.

Every time we hear a word from God but fail to obey it, our hearts become hardened. A hard heart develops the same way as a callus on the hand: It doesn't happen all at once; it forms one layer at a time. This is how we become calloused, or insensitive, to God. Every time God leads us to do something and we don't obey, it decreases our sensitivity by one layer. If we ignore God's leading enough, we will eventually think we can't hear His voice anymore. Even though our hearts will become hardened, God will never stop speaking to us. Jesus said, *"My sheep hear my voice, and I know them, and they follow me"* (John 10:27). The Lord is always leading us and giving us instruction, but we need to be sensitive to it and act on it.

You may not have the tenth step of God's plan yet, but you know step one. God has put something on your heart. I'm sure there are reasons you haven't followed through on whatever He has told you to do, but whatever the reasons are, they aren't good enough. God loves you whether you follow His leading or not. Being obedient doesn't make God love you more; failing to obey doesn't make Him love you less. But God can't lead and direct you into His blessings and fulfillment without your cooperation.

Once He tells you to do something and gives you direction, you need to act on it. God has given you everything you need to live a victorious life and see His will fulfilled in your life (2 Pet. 1:3-4). You simply need to act on His Word and His leading.

OUTLINE • 11.3

VI. Many Christians let their feelings control how they act instead of letting faith steer them.

    A. Seeing God's will fulfilled in your life means learning to obey Him no matter how you feel.

    B. Trust God and follow His leading.

    C. He will never lead you to do something you can't do or something that isn't in your best interest.

    D. You can always do what God is asking you to do—you may lack the motivation, but you *can* do it if you really want to.

    E. This modern culture is always trying to shift the blame onto someone else or some exterior circumstance—anything other than accepting responsibility themselves.

    F. To fulfill God's will, you have to accept responsibility in your life.

    G. You are a person created in the image of God; therefore, you are responsible for your actions.

    H. God commanded believers: *"Rejoice in the Lord alway: and again I say, Rejoice"* (Phil. 4:4).

    I. God would be unjust to command you to *"rejoice in the Lord alway"* if it wasn't possible.

    J. You don't have to feel joy to rejoice in the Lord, because you always have joy in your spirit, whether you can feel it or not (Gal. 5:22).

        i. You can do what God tells you to do regardless of how you feel.

        ii. Rejoicing is like putting a bucket down into the well of life in your spirit and drawing out the fullness of God.

    K. Emotions should be like the caboose on a train—going wherever the train goes—but not determining anything.

VII. Elijah received a word from God and acted on it.

And Elijah the Tishbite, who was of the inhabitants of Gilead, said unto Ahab, As the Lord God of Israel liveth, before whom I stand, there shall not be dew nor rain these years, but according to my word.

1 KINGS 17:1

    A. He could have focused on the dangers to himself, but instead, he was obedient to the Lord—he received a word from God and *acted* on it.

    B. Elijah became the most dominant man in the entire nation because he received direction from God and acted on it.

C. Immediately after Elijah prophesied the drought, God gave him further direction:

Get thee hence, and turn thee eastward, and hide thyself by the brook Cherith, that is before Jordan. [4] And it shall be, that thou shalt drink of the brook; and I have commanded the ravens to feed thee there. [5] So he went and did according unto the word of the LORD.

1 KINGS 17:3-5A

D. God gave Elijah a promise of protection, but notice that the promise to provide for Elijah didn't come until *after* he obeyed His first instruction.

E. This is why so many people don't fulfill God's will for their lives—God reveals His will, but people start trying to rationalize how everything is going to work out before they act on what He has told them to do.

F. God sent Elijah's provision *there*—not where Elijah was but where God told him to go.

    i.   Also, notice that God had already commanded the provision.

    ii. Likewise, God doesn't send your provision to *you*; He sends your provision to where He told you to *go*.

    iii. You can't make following God's leading conditional upon seeing His provision first.

    iv. One reason you might not be seeing God's provision in your life is because you are too much *here* and not enough *there*.

G. Many born-again, Spirit-filled believers look at their lives and only see problems—they don't understand that they have the same power on the inside of them that raised Jesus Christ from the dead (Eph. 1:18-20).

H. *God's power isn't out in heaven someplace—it's on the inside of you.*

I. Instead of looking for a "fresh" word from God to fix your problem, act on the direction He has already given you in Scripture.

J. Every time you hear a word from God but fail to obey it, your heart becomes hardened.

K. Even though your heart will become hardened, God will never stop speaking to you (John 10:27).

L. Being obedient doesn't make God love you more; failing to obey doesn't make Him love you less—but God can't lead and direct you into His blessings and fulfillment without your cooperation.

M. God has given you everything you need to live a victorious life and see His will fulfilled in your life (2 Pet. 1:3-4)—you simply need to act on His Word and His leading.

6. Many Christians let their feelings control how they act instead of letting faith steer them. Seeing God's will fulfilled in your life means learning to obey Him no matter how you feel. Trust God and follow His leading. He will never lead you to do something you can't do or something that isn't in your best interest. You can always do what God is asking you to do—you may lack the motivation, but you *can* do it if you really want to. This modern culture is always trying to shift the blame onto someone else or some exterior circumstance—anything other than accepting responsibility themselves. To fulfill God's will, you have to accept responsibility in your life. You are a person created in the image of God; therefore, you are responsible for your actions. God commanded believers: *"Rejoice in the Lord alway: and again I say, Rejoice"* (Phil. 4:4). God would be unjust to command you to *"rejoice in the Lord alway"* if it wasn't possible. You don't have to feel joy to rejoice in the Lord, because you always have joy in your spirit, whether you can feel it or not (Gal. 5:22). You can do what God tells you to do regardless of how you feel. Rejoicing is like putting a bucket down into the well of life in your spirit and drawing out the fullness of God. Emotions should be like the caboose on a train—going wherever the train goes—but not determining anything.

6a. Does seeing God's will fulfilled in your life mean learning to obey Him no matter what?
Yes

6b. He will never lead you to do something you can't do or something that isn't in your

_____ _____.
    A. Best interest
    B. Game plan
    C. Life goals
    D. All of the above
    E. None of the above
    A. Best interest

6c. Discussion question: Why or why not do you agree with the statement "You can always do what God is asking you to do—you may lack the motivation, but you *can* do it if you really want to"?
Discussion question

6d. What did God command believers in Philippians 4:4?
"Rejoice in the Lord alway: and again I say, Rejoice"

6e. Discussion question: What things in your life have you allowed to be determined by your emotions? Do you think any changes need to be made in those areas?
Discussion question

7. Elijah received a word from God and acted on it (1 Kin. 17:1). He could have focused on the dangers to himself, but instead, he was obedient to the Lord—he received a word from God and *acted* on it. Elijah became the most dominant man in the entire nation because he received direction from God and acted on it. Immediately after Elijah prophesied the drought, God gave him further direction (1 Kin. 17:3-5a). God gave Elijah a promise of protection, but notice that the promise to provide for Elijah didn't come until *after* he obeyed His first instruction. This is why so many people don't fulfill God's will for their lives—God reveals His will, but people start trying to rationalize how everything is going to work out before they act on what He has told them to do. God sent Elijah's provision *there*—not where Elijah was but where God told him to go. Also, notice that God had already commanded the provision. Likewise, God doesn't send your provision to *you*; He sends your provision to where He told you to *go*. You can't make following God's leading conditional upon seeing His provision first. One reason you might not be seeing God's provision in your life is because you are too much *here* and not enough *there*. Many born-again, Spirit-filled believers look at their lives and only see problems—they don't understand that they have the same power on the inside of them that raised Jesus Christ from the dead (Eph. 1:18-20). *God's power isn't out in heaven someplace—it's on the inside of you.* Instead of looking for a "fresh" word from God to fix your problem, act on the direction He has already given you in Scripture. Every time you hear a word from God but fail to obey it, your heart becomes hardened. Even though your heart will become hardened, God will never stop speaking to you (John 10:27). Being obedient doesn't make God love you more; failing to obey doesn't make Him love you less—but God can't lead and direct you into His blessings and fulfillment without your cooperation. God has given you everything you need to live a victorious life and see His will fulfilled in your life (2 Pet. 1:3-4)—you simply need to act on His Word and His leading.

7a. How did Elijah become the most dominant man in the entire nation?
He received direction from God and acted on it

7b. Where did God send Elijah's provision?
***There*—where God told him to go**

7c. Can you make following God's leading conditional upon seeing His provision first?
No

7d. Discussion question: Do you think the idea that "one reason you might not be seeing God's provision in your life is because you are too much *here* and not enough *there*" applies to your life? If so, how?
Discussion question

7e. True or False: Even though your heart will become hardened, God will never stop speaking to you (John 10:27).
True

24. Does seeing God's will fulfilled in your life mean learning to obey Him no matter what?

_____

_____

_____

25. He will never lead you to do something you can't do or something that isn't in your
   _____ _____.
   A. Best interest
   B. Game plan
   C. Life goals
   D. All of the above
   E. None of the above

26. Discussion question: Why or why not Do you agree with the statement "You can always do what God is asking you to do—you may lack the motivation, but you *can* do it if you really want to"?

_____

_____

_____

27. What did God command believers in Philippians 4:4?

_____

_____

_____

28. Discussion question: What things in your life have you allowed to be determined by your emotions? Do you think any changes need to be made in those areas?

_____

_____

_____

29. How did Elijah become the most dominant man in the entire nation?

_____

_____

_____

30. Where did God send Elijah's provision?

_____

_____

_____

31. Can you make following God's leading conditional upon seeing His provision first?

_____

_____

_____

32. Discussion question: Do you think the idea that "one reason you might not be seeing God's provision in your life is because you are too much *here* and not enough *there*" applies to your life? If so, how?

_____

_____

_____

33. True or False: Even though your heart will become hardened, God will never stop speaking to you (John 10:27).

24. Yes
25. A. Best interest
26. *Discussion question*
27. *"Rejoice in the Lord always: and again I say, Rejoice"*
28. *Discussion question*
29. He received direction from God and acted on it
30. *There*—where God told him to go
31. No
32. *Discussion question*
33. True

PHILIPPIANS 4:4

Rejoice in the Lord alway: and again I say, Rejoice.

JOHN 16:33

These things I have spoken unto you, that in me ye might have peace. In the world ye shall have tribulation: but be of good cheer; I have overcome the world.

GALATIANS 5:22

But the fruit of the Spirit is love, joy, peace, longsuffering, gentleness, goodness, faith.

1 KINGS 17:1

And Elijah the Tishbite, who was of the inhabitants of Gilead, said unto Ahab, As the Lord God of Israel liveth, before whom I stand, there shall not be dew nor rain these years, but according to my word.

1 KINGS 18:10

As the Lord thy God liveth, there is no nation or kingdom, whither my lord hath not sent to seek thee: and when they said, He is not there; he took an oath of the kingdom and nation, that they found thee not.

1 KINGS 17:3-5

Get thee hence, and turn thee eastward, and hide thyself by the brook Cherith, that is before Jordan. [4] And it shall be, that thou shalt drink of the brook; and I have commanded the ravens to feed thee there. [5] So he went and did according unto the word of the Lord: for he went and dwelt by the brook Cherith, that is before Jordan.

EPHESIANS 1:18-20

The eyes of your understanding being enlightened; that ye may know what is the hope of his calling, and what the riches of the glory of his inheritance in the saints, [19] And what is the exceeding greatness of his power to us-ward who believe, according to the working of his mighty power, [20] Which he wrought in Christ, when he raised him from the dead, and set him at his own right hand in the heavenly places.

ISAIAH 28:11-12

For with stammering lips and another tongue will he speak to this people. [12] To whom he said, This is the rest wherewith ye may cause the weary to rest; and this is the refreshing: yet they would not hear.

JOHN 10:27

My sheep hear my voice, and I know them, and they follow me.

2 PETER 1:3-4

According as his divine power hath given unto us all things that pertain unto life and godliness, through the knowledge of him that hath called us to glory and virtue: [4] Whereby are given unto us exceeding great and precious promises: that by these ye might be partakers of the divine nature, having escaped the corruption that is in the world through lust.

PATIENT
ENDURANCE

LESSON 12.1

In our culture, we want what we want—and we want it *right now*. Most people are so short term in their thinking that they go for the immediate fix in every situation. Many people are in debt up to their eyeballs because they buy things on borrowed time, without considering the long-term consequences. Rather than buying used cars that would meet their needs, they go out and buy brand-new, expensive cars, which end up costing two-and-a-half times the original price tag after paying six years of interest! It all boils down to impatience. People are unwilling to wait and save money; they have to satisfy their cravings immediately. Even in the spiritual realm, very few people have patience.

The human tendency is to quit, fail, and give up. People can't wait. It's not human nature to wait. The strongest, best, and fittest of all are going to fail. In our own selves, we don't have what it takes to overcome. God, on the other hand, doesn't get weary. God doesn't faint. He never gives up. Patience is a God quality, not a human quality. Only through God can we obtain patience and endurance.

> *He giveth power to the faint; and to them that have no might he increaseth strength. [30] Even the youths shall faint and be weary, and the young men shall utterly fall: [31] But they that wait upon the LORD shall renew their strength; they shall mount up with wings as eagles; they shall run, and not be weary; and they shall walk, and not faint.*
>
> ISAIAH 40:29-31

The passage says, *"They that wait upon the LORD shall renew their strength."* This isn't talking about waiting like hanging around waiting for a bus or a train. Waiting on the Lord is more than just killing time until something happens. It's more like a waiter at a good restaurant who watches to see if we need anything. "Can I get you more water? Is there anything else I can help you with?" This is exactly how we need to wait upon the Lord: watching, looking, and searching for ways to help. In order to fulfill God's purposes, we need Him to work His patience on the inside of us. *We need God's ability to endure* because it is not human nature to be patient or persistent—we hate waiting and we're prone to give up when things get tough.

Sometimes when I teach this at Charis Bible College, people get upset. Some people have the attitude that they don't need to wait because they think God is going to do things for them instantly. Some have quit school before they graduate because they were so adamant about needing to do something *right now*. In most cases, years and years have passed and they still haven't done anything. They would have been better off to be patient and let God work in their lives to prepare them.

Even if someone finds God's will and starts following it, the tendency for them to stick with it for a prolonged period of time is slim. I have seen this happen with ministers and people in every walk of life. I have seen so many people come and go, who initially had a zeal for God but couldn't maintain it. The Christian life is a marathon, not a sprint. Some people start the race well, pulling out ahead early—but they don't have any endurance. They stand for a short while but then give up. This is a major problem in the body of Christ.

Resist Problems

I believe there has been a lot of wrong teaching about how to gain patience and endure in the Christian walk. Many preachers are teaching that tribulation and hardship will teach you patience. Often they will quote the scripture that says tribulation *works* patience (Rom. 5:3), but that scripture means *work* in the sense of "exercise." Tribulation does not *create* patience.

If hardship made people patient, then those who have suffered the most hardship would automatically be the most patient. But this isn't the case. Often the people who have the most problems are the least patient people you will ever meet. Patience doesn't come from problems. Tribulation only gives you the opportunity to grow and exercise patience.

Patience is simply faith over a prolonged period of time. Momentary faith is something you can build up in a person by encouraging them; patience is long-term faith that doesn't waver. It stays consistent over a prolonged period of time. Plenty of people feel faith when they first get started walking with God, but they can't seem to maintain it.

The fruit of the Spirit is love, joy, peace, long-suffering, gentleness, goodness, faith, meekness, and temperance (Gal. 5:22-23). Long-suffering means patience—patience is actually a fruit of the Holy Spirit. When you are born again, God gives you patience. But you have to do something to activate it. Scripture says that faith comes by hearing and hearing by the Word of God (Rom. 10:17). Patience is built up within you as you study the Word of God.

When tough situations or trials come against you, they give you an opportunity to grow and develop in your faith—but faith must already be in you through the Word and through what God has put in your heart. Embracing problems is not going to help you. You have to resist problems. The teaching that says that God puts problems in your life to make you patient or stronger is completely wrong. Satan puts problems in your life to steal the Word (Mark 4:15). But if you stand on the Word in the midst of your problems and keep doing what God tells you to do, you will become stronger in faith and patience. This is the manner in which tribulation *works* patience. Patience is important in the Christian walk, but it doesn't come through hardship—it comes through the Word of God (Rom. 15:4).

Keep at It

And we desire that every one of you do shew the same diligence to the full assurance of hope unto the end: [12] That ye be not slothful, but followers of them who through faith and patience inherit the promises.

HEBREWS 6:11-12

In contrast to being slothful or lazy, we are encouraged to be followers of those who by faith and patience inherit the promises. Faith and patience take a lot of effort. You have to seek God. You have to be proactive about turning off other things that draw your attention away and numb you to God. It takes commitment. This is one of the reasons that coming to Bible school is so important for a lot of people—it's a major commitment. It costs money, effort, and a couple years of one's life. When you put effort into something, you get more out of it.

Countless people's lives consist of getting up, going to work, coming home, watching television, and going to bed—then doing the whole thing all over again the next day, like a little hamster on a wheel going around and around. They aren't seeking God; they don't know what His Word says—they're getting nowhere in fulfilling His purpose for their lives. Inheriting the promises takes effort. You have to make a commitment to seek God.

Remaining constant is also important. We can't go in spurts, seeking the Lord when trouble is staring us in the face and then going back to carnal living as soon as the pressure is off. Carnal living is what produces problems in the first place! Living for God is the solution, but it takes effort on our part.

Nature tends toward a state of decline. It's easier to be fat than it is to stay skinny. It's easier to be sick than it is to get well. It's easier to float downstream than it is to swim upstream. We have to fight against the problems and sicknesses that try to come against us in life. A lot of people think they don't have any control over these things—but they do. *You* resist the devil, and he will flee from *you* (James 4:7).

Arthritis doesn't come on you all at once like a seizure. You don't wake up one morning and—*boom*—you have full-blown arthritis. It comes one little joint at a time. At first you accept it because it is only a little stiffness in one joint—you can live with that. You let it in, bit by bit, and before you know it, arthritis has riddled your entire body. That's exactly how sin works. That's how the devil operates. He sneaks up on you little by little, bit by bit, temptation by temptation. It takes diligence for you to have the faith and patience necessary to resist the attacks of the Enemy and stay in the Word of God.

Abraham had to patiently endure in order to inherit the promise God made to him. God made a promise to Abraham that he would be the father of many nations. Abraham had faith in what he heard. Faith comes by hearing, and hearing by the Word of God (Rom. 10:17). Abraham had a promise that he anchored his faith to, and after he had patiently endured, he obtained the promise (Heb. 6:13-15). But it took a long time. Abraham was about 86 years old when God promised him that his descendants would outnumber the stars in the sky (Gen. 15:4-5), but his son Isaac wasn't born until he was 100 (Gen. 21:5). How many of us would have waited on a promise that long? Most people would think God didn't come through for them unless something happens within the first *five seconds* of praying.

We need to realize that it often takes time to see God's will come to pass—especially outside of healing and other areas when an immediate miracle is needed. Trying to find and fulfill God's will for your life is a process. God can't take you from where you are to where you are supposed to be, all in one step.

The Lord spoke to me on July 26, 1999, and told me I was just beginning my ministry. Wow! That was discouraging and encouraging all at the same time. I had started ministering in 1968. I was thirty-one years into ministry when the Lord said I was just beginning. He said if I had died or stopped before going on television January 3, 2000, I would have missed my ministry. It's not that I had been out of the will of God; I had just been in preparation for thirty-one years. I was just entering into His perfect will (Rom. 12:2).

The Lord spoke to me on January 31, 2002, and told me I was limiting Him by my small thinking. When I changed my thinking, the results were miraculous. We had about 30 employees at the time; now we have over 230. At that time, we were reaching 6 percent or less of the United States with our *Gospel Truth* television program; now we have the potential of reaching *100* percent. More than 2 billion people around the world are able to watch our program. This all started happening more than thirty years *after* I entered into ministry. I'm fulfilling God's will step by step. It takes time, so we need to have patience not to give up along the way.

Look unto Jesus

Wherefore seeing we also are compassed about with so great a cloud of witnesses, let us lay aside every weight, and the sin which doth so easily beset us, and let us run with patience the race that is set before us, [2] Looking unto Jesus the author and finisher of our faith; who for the joy that was set before him endured the cross, despising the shame, and is set down at the right hand of the throne of God.

HEBREWS 12:1-2

Patience will keep us going day after day and year after year. It's how we endure. We get it by looking unto Jesus, the Author and Finisher of our faith. Patience is a fruit of the Spirit (Gal. 5:22). It comes through the Word of God (Rom. 15:4). Jesus is the Word of God (John 1:1 and 14), both living and written—therefore, fruit comes through a personal relationship with God. This amplifies another problem in many believers' lives: They honestly don't have a vibrant, life-giving relationship with Jesus. They know Him from a distance. When we have a good relationship with God, not only do we talk to Him, but we also hear His voice when He speaks to us.

A great example of the importance of staying focused on Jesus is given in the Gospel of Matthew when Peter walked on water (Matt. 14:29). They were out in a boat, in the middle of a large body of water, in rough seas, when Jesus came walking to them on the water. Peter said, "Lord, if it's You, bid me come unto You on the water." And Jesus said, "Come." So, Peter got out of the boat and started walking on the water. It was miraculous.

But after walking a little way, he took his eyes off Jesus and started paying attention to the wind and the waves. When he did this, he began to sink. Think about that for a moment. The wind and the waves had absolutely nothing to do with Peter's ability to walk on water! He couldn't have walked on water even if the sea was smooth as glass. The weather had nothing to do with it. Peter took his attention off of Jesus, the Author and Finisher of his faith, and started focusing on his circumstances. When he did that, he began to sink.

It is notable that Peter didn't sink all at once. He just *began* to sink. In the same way, we don't lose our faith all at once. We don't get impatient all at once; it happens gradually. It is usually so gradual that we don't even realize we are taking our attention off Jesus and looking at other things. We seek Jesus when our situations are impossible and we absolutely must have a miracle, but when things are going well, we take our attention off Him. We relax. That's when we get into trouble. Scripture goes on to tell us how to avoid this downfall:

> *For consider him that endured such contradiction of sinners against himself, lest ye be wearied and faint in your minds.*
>
> HEBREWS 12:3

Fainting—the loss of strength or enthusiasm—begins in the mind. This is where the "sinking" begins. We have to guard our thoughts because Satan comes to us through our thinking. As a man thinks in his heart, so is he (Prov. 23:7). We have to focus our thoughts and attention on Jesus. The sad fact is that most of us have allowed the cares of this life, the deceitfulness of riches, and the lust of other things to turn our attention away from the Lord and choke out His power in our lives (Mark 4:19). The reason we don't have patience is because we are focusing on the world and the instant gratification it offers. We aren't looking to the Lord.

If this is a problem for you, then the solution is simple: Focus on Jesus, not your circumstances. Seek God with your whole heart. Keep your relationship with Him strong and you will endure. I have a course that I teach in our Bible school entitled "Longevity in Ministry," which focuses on maintaining a vibrant relationship with God. Fulfilling God's will is all about relationship. If you keep your relationship with God red hot, you will endure. You won't understand everything and you'll make some mistakes, but God will always show you the way to go when you are in relationship with Him.

Many seek what God has to offer, but they don't seek God Himself. When they are in a crisis, they seek Him. But when things are going well, they take their eyes off Jesus and begin to sink. Our goal should be to seek a relationship with God first; then everything else will be given to us.

OUTLINE • 12.1

I. Patience is a God quality, not a human quality.

    A. Only through God can we obtain patience and endurance.

    He giveth power to the faint; and to them that have no might he increaseth strength. [30] Even the youths shall faint and be weary, and the young men shall utterly fall: [31] But they that wait upon the LORD shall renew their strength; they shall mount up with wings as eagles; they shall run, and not be weary; and they shall walk, and not faint.

    ISAIAH 40:29-31

    B. Waiting on the Lord is more than just killing time until something happens.

    C. We need to wait upon the Lord by watching, looking, and searching for ways to help.

    D. *We need God's ability to endure* because it is not human nature to be patient or persistent—we hate waiting and we're prone to give up when things get tough.

    E. The Christian life is a marathon, not a sprint.

    F. Some people start the race well, pulling out ahead early—but they don't have any endurance.

    G. This is a major problem in the body of Christ.

II. Many preachers will quote the scripture that says tribulation *works* patience (Rom. 5:3), but that scripture means *work* in the sense of "exercise"—tribulation does not *create* patience.

    A. Tribulation only gives you the opportunity to grow and exercise patience.

    B. *Patience is simply faith over a prolonged period of time.*

    C. Momentary faith is something you can build up in a person by encouraging them; patience is long-term faith that doesn't waver.

    D. When you are born again, God gives you patience (Gal. 5:22-23), but you have to do something to activate it (Rom. 10:17).

    E. When tough situations or trials come against you, they give you an opportunity to grow and develop in your faith—but faith must already be in you through the Word and through what God has put in your heart.

    F. Embracing problems is not going to help you.

    G. Satan puts problems in your life to steal the Word (Mark 4:15).

    H. Patience is important in the Christian walk, but it doesn't come through hardship—it comes through the Word of God (Rom. 15:4).

III. In contrast to being slothful or lazy, believers are encouraged to be followers of those who by faith and patience inherit the promises.

> *And we desire that every one of you do shew the same diligence to the full assurance of hope unto the end: [12] That ye be not slothful, but followers of them who through faith and patience inherit the promises.*
>
> HEBREWS 6:11-12

A. Faith and patience take a lot of effort.

B. When you put effort into something, you get more out of it.

C. You have to make a commitment to seek God.

D. Remaining constant is also important.

E. Nature tends toward a state of decline.

F. A lot of people think they don't have any control—but they do: *You* resist the devil, and he will flee from *you* (James 4:7).

G. It takes diligence for you to have the faith and patience necessary to resist the attacks of the Enemy and stay in the Word of God (Rom. 10:17).

H. Abraham had a promise that he anchored his faith to, and after he had patiently endured, he obtained the promise (Heb. 6:13-15), but it took a long time (Gen. 15:4-5 and 21:5).

I. You need to realize that it often takes time to see God's will come to pass—especially outside of healing and other areas when an immediate miracle is needed.

J. Trying to find and fulfill God's will for your life is a process.

K. It takes time, so you need to have patience not to give up along the way.

IV. Patience will keep us going day after day and year after year—it's how we endure.

> *Wherefore seeing we also are compassed about with so great a cloud of witnesses, let us lay aside every weight, and the sin which doth so easily beset us, and let us run with patience the race that is set before us, [2] Looking unto Jesus the author and finisher of our faith; who for the joy that was set before him endured the cross, despising the shame, and is set down at the right hand of the throne of God.*
>
> HEBREWS 12:1-2

A. We get it by looking unto Jesus, the Author and Finisher of our faith.

    i. Patience is a fruit of the Spirit (Gal. 5:22).

    ii. It comes through the Word of God (Rom. 15:4).

    iii. Jesus is the Word of God (John 1:1 and 14), both living and written—therefore, fruit comes through a personal relationship with God.

B. When we have a good relationship with God, not only do we talk to Him, but we also hear His voice when He speaks to us.

C. A great example of the importance of staying focused on Jesus is given in the Gospel of Matthew when Peter walked on water (Matt. 14:29).

    i. Peter took his attention off of Jesus, the Author and Finisher of his faith, and started focusing on his circumstances.

    ii. When he did that, he began to sink.

D. It is notable that Peter didn't sink all at once; he just *began* to sink.

E. In the same way, we don't lose our faith or get impatient all at once.

F. It is usually so gradual that we don't even realize we are taking our attention off Jesus and looking at other things.

G. Scripture goes on to tell us how to avoid this downfall:

For consider him that endured such contradiction of sinners against himself, lest ye be wearied and faint in your minds.

HEBREWS 12:3

H. We have to guard our thoughts because Satan comes to us through our thinking (Prov. 23:7).

I. The sad fact is that most of us have allowed the cares of this life, the deceitfulness of riches, and the lust of other things to turn our attention away from the Lord and choke out His power in our lives (Mark 4:19).

J. If this is a problem for us, then the solution is simple: We should focus on Jesus, not our circumstances.

K. Many seek what God has to offer, but they don't seek God Himself.

L. Our goal should be to seek a relationship with God first; then everything else will be given to us.

1. Patience is a God quality, not a human quality. Only through God can we obtain patience and endurance.

> *He giveth power to the faint; and to them that have no might he increaseth strength. [30] Even the youths shall faint and be weary, and the young men shall utterly fall: [31] But they that wait upon the Lord shall renew their strength; they shall mount up with wings as eagles; they shall run, and not be weary; and they shall walk, and not faint.*
>
> ISAIAH 40:29:31

Waiting on the Lord is more than just killing time until something happens. We need to wait upon the Lord by watching, looking, and searching for ways to help. *We need God's ability to endure* because it is not human nature to be patient or persistent—we hate waiting and we're prone to give up when things get tough. The Christian life is a marathon, not a sprint. Some people start the race well, pulling out ahead early—but they don't have any endurance. This is a major problem in the body of Christ.

1a. Is patience a God quality or a human quality?
A God quality

1b. Isaiah 40:29-31 says, *"He giveth power to the faint; and to them that have no might he increaseth _____. [30] Even the youths shall _____ and be weary, and the young men shall utterly fall: [31] But they that _____ upon the Lord shall renew their strength; they shall mount up with wings as eagles; they shall run, and not be weary; and they shall walk, and not faint."*
"Strength" / "faint" / "wait"

1c. Discussion question: What does waiting on the Lord mean to you?
Discussion question

1d. Discussion question: Why do you think some people start their race well but don't finish?
Discussion question

2. Many preachers will quote the scripture that says tribulation *works* patience (Rom. 5:3), but that scripture means *work* in the sense of "exercise"—tribulation does not *create* patience. Tribulation only gives you the opportunity to grow and exercise patience. *Patience is simply faith over a prolonged period of time.* Momentary faith is something you can build up in a person by encouraging them; patience is long-term faith that doesn't waver. When you are born again, God gives you patience (Gal. 5:22-23), but you have to do something to activate it (Rom. 10:17). When tough situations or trials come against you, they give you an opportunity to grow and develop in your faith—but faith must already be in you through the Word and through what God has put in your heart. Embracing problems is not going to help you. Satan puts problems in your life to steal the Word (Mark 4:15). Patience is important in the Christian walk, but it doesn't come through hardship—it comes through the Word of God (Rom. 15:4).

2a. True or false: Tribulation creates patience.
   False

2b. Patience is simply faith over what?
   A. Your circumstances
   B. A prolonged period of time
   C. The next ten minutes
   D. All of the above
   E. None of the above
   B. A prolonged period of time

2c. Discussion question: How have you used tough situations and trials as opportunities to grow and develop in your faith?
   Discussion question

2d. If patience doesn't come though hardship, where does it come from?
   Through the Word of God (Rom. 15:4)

3. In contrast to being slothful or lazy, believers are encouraged to be followers of those who by faith and patience inherit the promises.

> *And we desire that every one of you do shew the same diligence to the full assurance of hope unto the end:* *[12]* *That ye be not slothful, but followers of them who through faith and patience inherit the promises.*
> HEBREWS 6:11-12

Faith and patience take a lot of effort. When you put effort into something, you get more out of it. You have to make a commitment to seek God. Remaining constant is also important. Nature tends toward a state of decline. A lot of people think they don't have any control—but they do: *You* resist the devil, and he will flee from *you* (James 4:7). It takes diligence for you to have the faith and patience necessary to resist the attacks of the Enemy and stay in the Word of God (Rom. 10:17). Abraham had a promise that he anchored his faith to, and after he had patiently endured, he obtained the promise (Heb. 6:13-15), but it took a long time (Gen. 15:4-5 and 21:5). You need to realize that it often takes time to see God's will come to pass—especially outside of healing and other areas when an immediate miracle is needed. Trying to find and fulfill God's will for your life is a process. It takes time, so you need to have patience not to give up along the way.

3a. Discussion question: Read Hebrews 6:11-12. How can you apply this passage to your life and walk with God? Give some examples of *"them who through faith and patience inherit the promises."*
   Discussion question

3b. What happens when you put effort into something?
   You get more out of it

3c. Discussion question: Have you put this principle (see #3b) to work in your life? Has it worked for you? In what ways?
   Discussion question

3d. Trying to find and fulfill God's will for your life is a _____.
   Process

4. Patience will keep us going day after day and year after year—it's how we endure.

Wherefore seeing we also are compassed about with so great a cloud of witnesses, let us lay aside every weight, and the sin which doth so easily beset us, and let us run with patience the race that is set before us, [2] Looking unto Jesus the author and finisher of our faith; who for the joy that was set before him endured the cross, despising the shame, and is set down at the right hand of the throne of God.
HEBREWS 12:1-2

We get it by looking unto Jesus, the Author and Finisher of our faith. Patience is a fruit of the Spirit (Gal. 5:22). It comes through the Word of God (Rom. 15:4). Jesus is the Word of God (John 1:1 and 14), both living and written—therefore, fruit comes through a personal relationship with God. When we have a good relationship with God, not only do we talk to Him, but we also hear His voice when He speaks to us. A great example of the importance of staying focused on Jesus is given in the Gospel of Matthew when Peter walked on water (Matt. 14:29). Peter took his attention off of Jesus, the Author and Finisher of his faith, and started focusing on his circumstances. When he did that, he began to sink. It is notable that Peter didn't sink all at once; he just *began* to sink. In the same way, we don't lose our faith or get impatient all at once. It is usually so gradual that we don't even realize we are taking our attention off Jesus and looking at other things. Scripture goes on to tell us how to avoid this downfall (Heb. 12:3). We have to guard our thoughts because Satan comes to us through our thinking (Prov. 23:7). The sad fact is that most of us have allowed the cares of this life, the deceitfulness of riches, and the lust of other things to turn our attention away from the Lord and choke out His power in our lives (Mark 4:19). If this is a problem for us, then the solution is simple: We should focus on Jesus, not our circumstances. Many seek what God has to offer, but they don't seek God Himself. Our goal should be to seek a relationship with God first; then everything else will be given to us.

4a. Discussion question: What does Hebrews 12:1-2 mean to you?
    Discussion question

4b. _____ is a fruit of the Spirit (Gal. 5:22).
    A. Patience
    B. Pineapple
    C. Passion fruit
    D. Pomegranate
    E. Productivity
    A. Patience

4c. What is a great example of the importance of staying focused on Jesus?
    Peter walking on water (Matt. 14:29)

4d. Discussion question: Why is this a great example (see #4c)? What can you learn from it?
    Discussion question

4e. Discussion question: "It is usually so gradual that we don't even realize we are taking our attention off Jesus and looking at other things." How has this happened to you and how did you deal with it?
    Discussion question

DISCIPLESHIP QUESTIONS • 12.1

1. Is patience a God quality or a human quality?

    _____

    _____

    _____

2. Isaiah 40:29-31 says, *"He giveth power to the faint; and to them that have no might
    he increaseth _____. [30] Even the youths shall _____ and
    be weary, and the young men shall utterly fall: [31] But they that _____ upon
    the* LORD *shall renew their strength; they shall mount up with wings as eagles; they shall
    run, and not be weary; and they shall walk, and not faint."*

3. Discussion question: What does waiting on the Lord mean to you?

    _____

    _____

    _____

4. Discussion question: Why do you think some people start their race well but don't finish?

    _____

    _____

    _____

5. True or false: Tribulation creates patience.

6. Patience is simply faith over what?
    A. Your circumstances
    B. A prolonged period of time
    C. The next ten minutes
    D. All of the above
    E. None of the above

7. Discussion question: How have you used tough situations and trials as opportunities to grow and develop in your faith?

    _____

    _____

    _____

8. If patience doesn't come though hardship, where does it come from?

    _____

    _____

    _____

9. Discussion question: Read Hebrews 6:11-12. How can you apply this passage to your life and walk with God? Give some examples of *"them who through faith and patience inherit the promises."*

    _____

    _____

    _____

10. What happens when you put effort into something?

    _____

    _____

    _____

11. Discussion question: Have you put this principle (see #10) to work in your life? Has it worked for you? In what ways?

    _____

    _____

    _____

12. Trying to find and fulfill God's will for your life is a _____.

13.   Discussion question: What does Hebrews 12:1-2 mean to you?

_____

_____

_____

14.   _____ is a fruit of the Spirit (Gal. 5:22).
      A. Patience
      B. Pineapple
      C. Passion fruit
      D. Pomegranate
      E. Productivity

15.   What is a great example of the importance of staying focused on Jesus?

_____

_____

_____

16.   Discussion question: Why is this a great example (see #15)? What can you learn from it?

_____

_____

_____

17.   Discussion question: "It is usually so gradual that we don't even realize we are taking our attention off Jesus and looking at other things." How has this happened to you and how did you deal with it?

_____

_____

_____

ANSWER KEY • 12.1

1. A God quality
2. *"Strength" / "faint" / "wait"*
3. *Discussion question*
4. *Discussion question*
5. False
6. B.   A prolonged period of time
7. *Discussion question*
8. Through the Word of God (Rom. 15:4)
9. *Discussion question*
10. You get more out of it
11. *Discussion question*
12. Process
13. *Discussion question*
14. A. Patience
15. Peter walking on water (Matt. 14:22-33)
16. *Discussion question*
17. *Discussion question*

ISAIAH 40:29-31
He giveth power to the faint; and to them that have no might he increaseth strength. [30] Even the youths shall faint and be weary, and the young men shall utterly fall: [31] But they that wait upon the Lord shall renew their strength; they shall mount up with wings as eagles; they shall run, and not be weary; and they shall walk, and not faint.

ROMANS 5:3
And not only so, but we glory in tribulations also: knowing that tribulation worketh patience.

GALATIANS 5:22-23
But the fruit of the Spirit is love, joy, peace, longsuffering, gentleness, goodness, faith, [23] Meekness, temperance: against such there is no law.

ROMANS 10:17
So then faith cometh by hearing, and hearing by the word of God.

MARK 4:15
And these are they by the way side, where the word is sown; but when they have heard, Satan cometh immediately, and taketh away the word that was sown in their hearts.

ROMANS 15:4
For whatsoever things were written aforetime were written for our learning, that we through patience and comfort of the scriptures might have hope.

HEBREWS 6:11-15
And we desire that every one of you do shew the same diligence to the full assurance of hope unto the end: [12] That ye be not slothful, but followers of them who through faith and patience inherit the promises. [13] For when God made promise to Abraham, because he could swear by no greater, he sware by himself, [14] Saying, Surely blessing I will bless thee, and multiplying I will multiply thee. [15] And so, after he had patiently endured, he obtained the promise.

JAMES 4:7
Submit yourselves therefore to God. Resist the devil, and he will flee from you.

GENESIS 15:4-5
And, behold, the word of the LORD came unto him, saying, This shall not be thine heir; but he that shall come forth out of thine own bowels shall be thine heir. [5] And he brought him forth abroad, and said, Look now toward heaven, and tell the stars, if thou be able to number them: and he said unto him, So shall thy seed be.

GENESIS 21:5
And Abraham was an hundred years old, when his son Isaac was born unto him.

ROMANS 12:2
And be not conformed to this world: but be ye transformed by the renewing of your mind, that ye may prove what is that good, and acceptable, and perfect, will of God.

HEBREWS 12:1-3
Wherefore seeing we also are compassed about with so great a cloud of witnesses, let us lay aside every weight, and the sin which doth so easily beset us, and let us run with patience the race that is set before us, [2] Looking unto Jesus the author and finisher of our faith; who for the joy that was set before him endured the cross, despising the shame, and is set down at the right hand of the throne of God. [3] For consider him that endured such contradiction of sinners against himself, lest ye be wearied and faint in your minds.

JOHN 1:1
In the beginning was the Word, and the Word was with God, and the Word was God.

JOHN 1:14
And the Word was made flesh, and dwelt among us, (and we beheld his glory, the glory as of the only begotten of the Father,) full of grace and truth.

MATTHEW 14:29

And he said, Come. And when Peter was come down out of the ship, he walked on the water, to go to Jesus.

PROVERBS 23:7

For as he thinketh in his heart, so is he: Eat and drink, saith he to thee; but his heart is not with thee.

MARK 4:19

And the cares of this world, and the deceitfulness of riches, and the lusts of other things entering in, choke the word, and it becometh unfruitful.

LESSON 12.2

In the previous lesson, I used Elijah as an example of someone who heard a word from God and acted on it. God did some truly great miracles through him because he was willing to be obedient. Elijah prophesied to King Ahab that there would be a drought (1 Kin. 17:1), and then disappeared for three years. When Elijah returned, he told Ahab to gather the entire nation of Israel together at Mount Carmel for a contest: 400 prophets of the grove and 450 prophets of Baal in a face-off against Elijah (1 Kin. 18:17-40). Elijah directed that they would each prepare an ox for sacrifice and then call for it to be consumed by fire. Then the true God would reveal Himself by sending fire from heaven to consume the sacrifice.

The prophets of the grove and the prophets of Baal called for fire from morning until late in the day, but nothing happened. While they were busy crying out to their false gods, Elijah mocked them, saying, "Maybe your god is talking to someone else, or he is on a journey, or maybe he's taking a nap and you should wake him." The false prophets became so desperate, they started cutting themselves.

When nothing happened by late afternoon, Elijah called for the people to draw near as he prepared his sacrifice. He built an altar out of twelve stones and then dug a trench around it. When the altar was built and the sacrifice was in place, he ordered the people to pour twelve barrels of water over the sacrifice and wood. Water soaked through the sacrifice, drenched the wood, and overflowed into the trenches Elijah had dug. Then Elijah called upon God to consume the sacrifice with fire. The Lord sent a fire from heaven that was so hot, it consumed the sacrifice, the wood, and the stone altar as well. When the people saw the consuming fire, they fell on their faces and said, "*The Lord, he is the God; the Lord, he is the God.*" (1 Kings 18:39b) Elijah had the people detain the false prophets—then he killed them.

After all that, Elijah told Ahab to eat and drink because Elijah could hear the sound of an abundance of rain. Then he went to the top of Mount Carmel to pray. The three-year drought was about to end. He prayed seven times, and finally a cloud, the size of a man's hand, appeared on the horizon. When that tiny cloud appeared, Elijah sent word to Ahab to prepare his chariot and head for home before he got stopped by the coming downpour. Shortly after Ahab departed, the drought was broken by a deluge. Elijah started running on foot to the same city and actually outran Ahab's chariot (1 Kin. 18:41-46). Elijah was pumped; his adrenaline was flowing.

Ahab's wife, Jezebel, was furious that Elijah had killed all of her false prophets. She sent a message to Elijah that said, *"So let the gods do to me, and more also, if I make not thy life as the life of one of them by to morrow about this time"* (1 Kin. 19:2). When Elijah saw this, he ran for his life. I don't doubt that Jezebel hated Elijah, but she was blowing smoke. She was threatening something she couldn't follow through with. Even tyrants have to consider the will of the people. The entire nation had seen fire fall from heaven at Elijah's word, so they wouldn't have let her kill Elijah.

If Jezebel had felt free to kill Elijah, she would have sent a soldier with a sword instead of a messenger with a note. She wanted Elijah dead, but she couldn't kill him. Her note was just intimidation, and that is exactly how the devil gets to us. He has no power over us, so he intimidates us. Then we defeat ourselves by running off in unbelief.

Jezebel said she was going to make Elijah like one of the 850 false prophets he had killed. Praise God, we live under a better covenant, and God doesn't deal with people like that anymore. But let's imagine what the scene looked like where Elijah killed 850 people. It must have been a gruesome picture. The scripture says that when Elijah *"saw"* (1 Kin. 19:3) what Jezebel had said to him, he ran. Her note brought the gruesome image to his mind, and he *saw* himself as one of the men he had just slain. He saw himself as a dead man. He had challenged the king and an entire nation, called down fire from heaven, and outran a chariot, but he was running from a woman with a note.

The Bible says that Elijah ran a day's journey into the wilderness, sat down under a juniper tree, and requested for God to take his life. He said, *"It is enough; now, O LORD, take away my life; for I am not better than my fathers"* (1 Kin. 19:4). Elijah's request reveals a lot. He wanted God to kill him because, he said, *"I am not better than my fathers."* He suddenly came to the conclusion that he wasn't any better than his forefathers, and it drove him into despair. This means that *prior* to this incident, he thought he *was* better than his forefathers.

Elijah had a string of unbroken successes. God protected him from Ahab during the three-year drought and supplied his needs supernaturally during that time. Elijah was the first man recorded in the Bible to see a person raised from the dead (1 Kin. 17:19-23). I know fifty or sixty people who have been raised from the dead. It's a relatively common thing today, but back then, nobody had ever heard of such a thing. Elijah was a powerful man of God. The problem was he started to believe he was someone special. He took his eyes off of God and began thinking it was his own power and ability that made all these miraculous things possible.

This story illustrates the point I'm making: You have to look unto Jesus, the Author and Finisher of your faith. You have to keep your attention on Him. Proverbs says that pride goes before destruction and a haughty spirit before a fall (Prov. 16:18). The moment you start patting yourself on the back and believing your own press releases, you are in trouble. It doesn't matter what you accomplish; you are still only a man or a woman.

It's like being in an airplane. People say, "I'm flying 500 miles an hour at 30,000 feet." No, you're not. The plane is flying—you're not. It's your position inside of the plane that keeps you airborne. If you don't believe it, then step outside of the plane and see what happens. You will plummet like a rock. In the same way, Christians aren't changing unbelievers' lives and causing miracles to happen. You aren't doing those things—God living in you is doing them. And if you ever take your attention off Jesus, the Author and Finisher of your faith, you are headed for a fall.

Elijah didn't have the patience to endure in this situation, because he got caught up in pride. Success ruined him. The same thing happens to us today. Not many people continue to seek God on the other side of a crisis—when everything is fine and their needs are met. As soon as they get whatever they were praying for, they go back to doing their own thing and begin the process of "sinking" all over again.

If you aren't careful, the circumstances of life will cause you to take your eyes off Jesus. For example, if somebody dies, all of a sudden, you take your attention off Jesus and begin to focus on your pain. As you do, you begin to sink. If your business fails and the financial pressure gets to you and you take your eyes off Jesus as the Provider of all your needs, you will begin to sink.

Patience is the ability to fix your attention on Jesus, not looking to the right-hand or to the left. It's the ability to remain unmoved by your circumstances. The only way I know how to get this kind of patience is by maintaining a close relationship with God through the Word. This sort of watchful vigilance is what it means to wait upon the Lord.

It doesn't matter if it has been ten years since God gave you major direction or if you are healthy and crisis free—stay focused on Jesus. God isn't going to speak life-changing words to you every day. He tells you He loves you and He gives you guidance, but He doesn't give you life-altering direction every day. Long stretches of time may pass when you are just studying the Word and doing what God told you to do last. That's okay—*patience* is faith over a prolonged period of time. Just do what God told you to do until He tells you differently.

Facing Adversity

After Elijah fell into pride, God tried to raise him up in the same way Jesus reached out His hand to Peter. He sent Elijah on a forty-day journey to Mount Horeb. When Elijah arrived there, he hid in a cave, and the voice of the Lord asked him, "What are you doing here, Elijah?" Instead of running away from Jezebel to hide in the wilderness, Elijah should have been leading the nation of Israel in the revival he started when he called down fire and killed the false prophets.

Elijah answered, *"I have been very jealous for the LORD God of hosts: for the children of Israel have forsaken thy covenant, thrown down thine altars, and slain thy prophets with the sword; and I, even I only, am left; and they seek my life, to take it away"* (1 Kin. 19:10). Elijah got caught up in self-pity and said something he knew was a lie. Right before Elijah told the king to assemble Israel before Mount Carmel, he met a man who had hidden 100 prophets of God and was keeping them safe (1 Kin. 18:13). Elijah knew that he wasn't the only prophet left alive.

This is what happens when you focus on your circumstances. You know things aren't really as bad as you think they are, but you get so focused on the problem that it becomes overwhelming. One person may wrong you, and you start complaining that nobody loves you and everything is going wrong. But it's not true and you know it; it's how you feel, so you indulge your flesh and start feeling sorry for yourself. You are headed for trouble once you start down that road. You need to get a grip on reality. You have to put things into perspective. Stop focusing on your problems, and start focusing on God. Jesus is the same yesterday, today, and forever. He doesn't change. If your life is based on Jesus, you will be happy when circumstances look bad, and you will be blessed when things look good. It won't matter either way; you will be consistent.

Elijah was way out of perspective, so God told him to go out and stand at the opening of the cave as He passed by. Three dramatic manifestations followed. A wind passed by that was so strong, it broke the rocks, but the Lord was not in the wind. After the wind, there came an earthquake, but the Lord was not in the earthquake. After the earthquake was a fire, but God was not in the fire either. Finally, Elijah heard a *still, small voice*, and it overwhelmed him so much that he wrapped his face in his cloak and went to stand at the opening of the cave (1 Kin. 19:11-13). Some people miss God because they look for Him in the spectacular. But God delights in faith, and we need to be listening for Him in the still, small voice that is on the inside of us.

God asked Elijah, "What are you doing here?" It is the exact same question He asked him the first time (1 Kin. 19:9). Here's a tip: If God asks you a question, you answer it, and then He asks you the exact same question again, it probably means you didn't get it right the first time. God is giving you a "do-over." Elijah didn't pick up on this, so he gave God the exact same answer. Elijah may have felt like the only prophet around, but he knew he wasn't. He was being dominated by his emotions. So, God told him to return to Damascus and anoint Hazael king over Syria, Jehu king over Israel, and Elisha to be prophet in his place (1 Kings 19:15-16). In other words, God told him to go find a replacement to carry on the ministry He needed someone to complete—since Elijah had given up.

Elijah only did one of the three things that God asked him to do. He anointed Elisha to replace him (1 Kin. 19:19-21), but he didn't do the other two things he heard God tell him in an audible voice. We know this because Elisha was the one who anointed Hazael king over Syria and Jehu king over Israel (2 Kin. 8:13 and 9:1-6).

Elijah checked out because he was depressed and discouraged. He didn't fulfill God's will for his life. Elijah was the first person to see someone raised from the dead (1 Kin. 17:17-23), and he experienced food being miraculously provided (1 Kin. 17:13-16). He also called fire down out of heaven and turned an entire nation to God (1 Kin. 18:38-39)! This is a prime example of how finishing is a lot harder than starting. Elijah did not fulfill God's purpose for his life, because he lost his focus. He got caught up in pride and took his attention off God—the Author and Finisher of his faith. He quit operating in patience.

Elijah missed it big time, but God still loved him. We have a tendency to think that God gets mad when we fail, because that's our experience in human relationships. But God doesn't operate that way. God didn't reject Elijah. In fact, Elijah's relationship with God was so strong that he never physically died. As Elijah and Elisha were walking together one day, a chariot of fire with horses of fire swooped down and took Elijah up to heaven in a whirlwind (2 Kin. 2:11). Elijah had such a strong relationship with God that he was one of two people who never physically died (Enoch was the other one, Gen. 5:24). God supernaturally translated him up into heaven.

Elijah's failure to carry out all the things God asked him to had consequences, but God didn't punish him. Ahab was supposed to be replaced as king by Jehu (1 Kin. 19:16), but he wasn't replaced, and terrible things happened as a result. Ahab killed Naboth (1 Kin. 21), which wouldn't have happened if Jehu had been king. The nation of Israel was in dire straits because Elijah didn't obey God, but God wasn't mad at him.

Even if you don't do everything that God calls you to do, His grace will still abound toward you (Rom. 5:20). God will still love you. You can still go to heaven without following God and doing everything He wants you to do. But our lives have a purpose. We have a job to do, and it isn't just about us being blessed. Who knows how things might have turned out if Elijah had obeyed God instead of falling into self-pity? We don't know what tragedies could have been avoided or what miracles might have come through him.

I have heard estimates that 80 percent of ministers today quit within the first five years of entering full-time ministry. What could they have accomplished if they had finished their course instead? A large percentage of those who remain in ministry are depressed and discouraged. What would happen if they knew how to operate in patience and look unto Jesus, the Author and Finisher of their faith? What would our world look like if every person who started the race was still in it and doing what God told them to do?

A lot of people start the race, but not many stay at it over the long haul. Finishing is more important than starting. You inherit the promises through faith and patience. You have to run with patience the race that is set before you, looking unto Jesus, not diverting your attention to the right-hand or to the left. When you are running a race, you can't go up into the grandstands and argue with the spectators; you might win the argument, but you are going to lose the race. Stay on track. Keep doing what God told you to do. Stay focused on Jesus, and don't get distracted by adverse circumstances in your life.

Make a commitment that you're going to love the Lord to the best of your ability. Determine now that you are going to keep running your race no matter what. Don't ever turn away from that commitment. Fulfilling God's will isn't for lazy Christians. You have to seek God with your whole heart—but it's worth it!

OUTLINE • 12.2

V. Elijah had a string of unbroken successes.

    A. He won a face-off against 850 false prophets, he then killed those 850 false prophets (1 Kin. 18:17-40), and he prophesied, prayed for, and saw the end of a three-year drought (1 Kin. 18:41-46).

    B. But he ended up running from Jezebel who'd threatened his life (1 Kin. 19:2).

    C. This left Elijah wanting God to kill him (1 Kin. 19:4).

    D. Elijah's story illustrates the point I'm making: You have to look unto Jesus, the Author and Finisher of your faith and keep your attention on Him (Prov. 16:18).

    E. The moment you start patting yourself on the back and believing your own press releases, you are in trouble—it doesn't matter what you accomplish; you are still only a man or a woman.

    F. You aren't doing those things—God living in you is doing them.

    G. Elijah didn't have the patience to endure in this situation, because he got caught up in pride.

    H. If you aren't careful, the circumstances of life will cause you to take your eyes off Jesus.

    I. Patience is the ability to fix your attention on Jesus, not looking to the right-hand or to the left—it's the ability to remain unmoved by your circumstances.

    J. Just do what God told you to do until He tells you differently.

VI. Like Elijah getting caught up in self-pity and saying something he knew was a lie (1 Kin. 19:10 and 18:13), this is what happens when you focus on your circumstances.

    A. You know things aren't really as bad as you think they are, but you get so focused on the problem that it becomes overwhelming.

    B. You have to put things into perspective: Stop focusing on your problems, and start focusing on God.

    C. Some people miss God because they look for Him in the spectacular—but God delights in faith, and you need to be listening for Him in the still, small voice that is on the inside of you (1 Kin. 19:11-13).

    D. Elijah did not fulfill God's purpose for his life, because he lost his focus (1 Kin. 19:15-17 and 19-21).

    E. He got caught up in pride and took his attention off God—the Author and Finisher of his faith; he quit operating in patience.

    F. Elijah missed it big time, but God still loved him (2 Kin. 2:11).

G. You may have a tendency to think that God gets mad when you fail, because that's your experience in human relationships, but God doesn't operate that way.

H. Even if you don't do everything that God calls you to do, His grace will still abound toward you (Rom. 5:20)—God will still love you.

I. But you have a job to do, and it isn't just about you being blessed.

J. A lot of people start the race, but not many stay at it over the long haul.

K. Finishing is more important than starting.

L. You inherit the promises through faith and patience.

M. Make a commitment that you're going to love the Lord to the best of your ability.

N. Determine now that you are going to keep running your race no matter what.

O. You have to seek God with your whole heart—but it's worth it!

5. Elijah had a string of unbroken successes. He won a face-off against 850 false prophets, he then killed those 850 false prophets (1 Kin. 18:17-40), and he prophesied, prayed for, and saw the end of a three-year drought (1 Kin. 18:41-46). But he ended up running from Jezebel who'd threatened his life (1 Kin. 19:2). This left Elijah wanting God to kill him (1 Kin. 19:4). Elijah's story illustrates the point I'm making: You have to look unto Jesus, the Author and Finisher of your faith and keep your attention on Him (Prov. 16:18). The moment you start patting yourself on the back and believing your own press releases, you are in trouble—it doesn't matter what you accomplish; you are still only a man or a woman. You aren't doing those things—God living in you is doing them. Elijah didn't have the patience to endure in this situation, because he got caught up in pride. If you aren't careful, the circumstances of life will cause you to take your eyes off Jesus. Patience is the ability to fix your attention on Jesus, not looking to the right-hand or to the left—it's the ability to remain unmoved by your circumstances. Just do what God told you to do until He tells you differently.

5a. Discussion question: What lessons can you learn from Elijah?
Discussion question

5b. True or false: The moment you start patting yourself on the back and believing your own press releases, you are in trouble.
True

5c. Why didn't Elijah have the patience to endure?
Because he got caught up in pride

5d. How long should you do what God told you to do?
Until He tells you differently

6. Like Elijah getting caught up in self-pity and saying something he knew was a lie (1 Kin. 19:10 and 18:13), this is what happens when you focus on your circumstances. You know things aren't really as bad as you think they are, but you get so focused on the problem that it becomes overwhelming. You have to put things into perspective: Stop focusing on your problems, and start focusing on God. Some people miss God because they look for Him in the spectacular—but God delights in faith, and you need to be listening for Him in the still, small voice that is on the inside of you (1 Kin. 19:11-13). Elijah did not fulfill God's purpose for his life, because he lost his focus (1 Kin. 19:15-17 and 19-21). He got caught up in pride and took his attention off God—the Author and Finisher of his faith; he quit operating in patience. Elijah missed it big time, but God still loved him (2 Kin. 2:11). You may have a tendency to think that God gets mad when you fail, because that's your experience in human relationships, but God doesn't operate that way. Even if you don't do everything that God calls you to do, His grace will still abound toward you (Rom. 5:20)—God will still love you. But you have a job to do, and it isn't just about you being blessed. A lot of people start the race, but not many stay at it over the long haul. Finishing is more important than starting. You inherit the promises through faith and patience. Make a commitment that you're going to love the Lord to the best of your ability. Determine now that you are going to keep running your race no matter what. You have to seek God with your whole heart—but it's worth it!

6a. Discussion question: Do you relate to the statement that "you know things aren't really as bad as you think they are, but you get so focused on the problem that it becomes overwhelming"? In what way? How did you resolve the situation?
Discussion question

6b. Some people miss God because they look for Him in the _____—but God _____ in faith, and we need to be _____ for Him in the still, small voice that is on the inside of us (1 Kin. 19:11-13).
Spectacular / delights / listening

6c. Did God stop loving Elijah even though he missed it big time (i.e., didn't fulfill God's purpose for his life)?
No

6d. Discussion question: In what ways, if any, do you think your experience in human relationships has influenced the way you relate to God?
Discussion question

6e. Even if you don't do everything God calls you to do, His grace will what?
   A. Leave and never come back
   B. Ignore you but stay around
   C. Still abound toward you
   D. All of the above
   E. None of the above
   C. Still abound toward you

18. Discussion question: What lessons can you learn from Elijah?

_____

_____

_____

19. True or false: The moment you start patting yourself on the back and believing your own press releases, you are in trouble.

20. Why didn't Elijah have the patience to endure?

_____

_____

_____

21. How long should you do what God told you to do?

_____

_____

_____

22. Discussion question: Do you relate to the statement that "you know things aren't really as bad as you think they are, but you get so focused on the problem that it becomes overwhelming"? In what way? How did you resolve the situation?

_____

_____

_____

23. Some people miss God because they look for Him in the _____—but God _____ in faith, and we need to be _____ for Him in the still, small voice that is on the inside of us (1 Kin. 19:11-13).

24. Did God stop loving Elijah even though he missed it big time (i.e., didn't fulfill God's purpose for his life)?

_____

_____

_____

25. Discussion question: In what ways, if any, do you think your experience in human relationships has influenced the way you relate to God?

_____

_____

_____

26. Even if you don't do everything God calls you to do, His grace will what?
    A. Leave and never come back
    B. Ignore you but stay around
    C. Still abound toward you
    D. All of the above
    E. None of the above

18. *Discussion question*
19. True
20. Because he got caught up in pride
21. Until He tells you differently
22. *Discussion question*
23. Spectacular / delights / listening
24. No
25. *Discussion question*
26. C. Still abound toward you

1 KINGS 17:1

And Elijah the Tishbite, who was of the inhabitants of Gilead, said unto Ahab, As the Lord God of Israel liveth, before whom I stand, there shall not be dew nor rain these years, but according to my word.

1 KINGS 18:17-46

And it came to pass, when Ahab saw Elijah, that Ahab said unto him, Art thou he that troubleth Israel? [18] And he answered, I have not troubled Israel; but thou, and thy father's house, in that ye have forsaken the commandments of the Lord, and thou hast followed Baalim. [19] Now therefore send, and gather to me all Israel unto mount Carmel, and the prophets of Baal four hundred and fifty, and the prophets of the groves four hundred, which eat at Jezebel's table. [20] So Ahab sent unto all the children of Israel, and gathered the prophets together unto mount Carmel. [21] And Elijah came unto all the people, and said, How long halt ye between two opinions? if the Lord be God, follow him: but if Baal, then follow him. And the people answered him not a word. [22] Then said Elijah unto the people, I, even I only, remain a prophet of the Lord; but Baal's prophets are four hundred and fifty men. [23] Let them therefore give us two bullocks; and let them choose one bullock for themselves, and cut it in pieces, and lay it on wood, and put no fire under: and I will dress the other bullock, and lay it on wood, and put no fire under: [24] And call ye on the name of your gods, and I will call on the name of the Lord: and the God that answereth by fire, let him be God. And all the people answered and said, It is well spoken. [25] And Elijah said unto the prophets of Baal, Choose you one bullock for yourselves, and dress it first; for ye are many; and call on the name of your gods, but put no fire under. [26] And they took the bullock which was given them, and they dressed it, and called on the name of Baal from morning even until noon, saying, O Baal, hear us. But there was no voice, nor any that answered. And they leaped upon the altar which was made. [27] And it came to pass at noon, that Elijah mocked them, and said, Cry aloud: for he is a god; either he is talking, or he is pursuing, or he is in a journey, or peradventure he sleepeth, and must be awaked. [28] And they cried aloud, and cut themselves after their manner with knives and lancets, till the blood gushed out upon them. [29] And it came to pass, when midday was past, and they prophesied until the time of the offering of the evening sacrifice, that there was neither voice, nor any to answer, nor any that regarded. [30] And Elijah said unto all the people, Come near unto me. And all the people came near unto him. And he repaired the altar of the Lord that was broken down. [31] And Elijah took twelve stones, according to the number of the tribes of the sons of Jacob, unto whom the word of the Lord came, saying, Israel shall be thy name: [32] And with the stones he built an altar in the name of the Lord: and he made a trench about the altar, as great as would contain two measures of seed. [33] And he put the wood in order, and cut the bullock in pieces, and laid him on the wood, and said, Fill four barrels with water, and pour it on the burnt sacrifice, and on the wood. [34] And he said, Do it the second time. And they did it the second time. And he said, Do it the third time. And they did it the third time. [35] And the water ran round about the altar; and he filled the trench also with water. [36] And it came to pass at the time of the offering of the evening sacrifice, that Elijah the prophet came near, and said, LORD God of Abraham, Isaac, and of Israel, let it be known this day that thou art God in Israel, and that I am thy servant, and that I have done all these things at thy word. [37] Hear me, O LORD, hear me, that this people may know that thou art the LORD God, and that thou hast turned their heart back again. [38] Then the fire of the LORD fell, and consumed the burnt sacrifice, and the wood, and the stones, and the dust, and licked up the water that was in the trench. [39] And when all the people saw it, they fell on their faces: and they said, The LORD, he is the God; the LORD, he is the God. [40] And Elijah said unto them, Take the prophets of Baal; let not one of them escape. And they took them: and Elijah brought them down to the brook Kishon, and slew them there. [41] And Elijah said unto Ahab, Get thee up, eat and drink; for there is a sound of abundance of rain. [42] So Ahab went up to eat and to drink. And Elijah went up to the top of Carmel; and he cast himself down upon the earth, and put his face between his knees, [43] And said to his servant, Go up now, look toward the sea. And he went up, and looked, and said, There is nothing. And he said, Go again seven times. [44] And it came to pass at the seventh time, that he said, Behold, there ariseth a little cloud out of the sea, like a man's hand. And he said, Go up, say unto Ahab, Prepare thy chariot, and get thee down, that the rain stop thee not. [45] And it came to pass in the mean while, that the heaven was black with clouds and wind, and there was a great rain. And Ahab rode, and went to Jezreel. [46] And the hand of the LORD was on Elijah; and he girded up his loins, and ran before Ahab to the entrance of Jezreel.

1 KINGS 19:2-4

Then Jezebel sent a messenger unto Elijah, saying, So let the gods do to me, and more also, if I make not thy life as the life of one of them by to morrow about this time. [3] And when he saw that, he arose, and went for his life, and came to Beersheba, which belongeth to Judah, and left his servant there. [4] But he himself went a day's journey into the wilderness, and came and sat down under a juniper tree: and he requested for himself that he might die; and said, It is enough; now, O LORD, take away my life; for I am not better than my fathers.

1 KINGS 17:13-23

And Elijah said unto her, Fear not; go and do as thou hast said: but make me thereof a little cake first, and bring it unto me, and after make for thee and for thy son. [14] For thus saith the LORD God of Israel, The barrel of meal shall not waste, neither shall the cruse of oil fail, until the day that the LORD sendeth rain upon the earth. [15] And she went and did according to the saying of Elijah: and she, and he, and her house, did eat many days. [16] And the barrel of meal wasted not, neither did the cruse of oil fail, according to the word of the LORD, which he spake by Elijah. [17] And it came to pass after these things, that the son of the woman, the mistress of the house, fell sick; and his sickness was so sore, that there was no breath left in him. [18] And she said unto Elijah, What have I to do with thee, O thou man of God? art thou come unto me to call my sin to remembrance, and to slay my son? [19] And he said unto her, Give me thy son. And he took him out of her bosom, and carried him up into a loft, where he abode, and laid him upon his own bed. [20] And he cried unto the LORD, and said, O LORD my God, hast thou also brought evil upon the widow with whom I sojourn, by slaying her son? [21] And he stretched himself upon the child three times, and cried unto the LORD, and said, O LORD my God, I pray thee, let this child's soul come into him again. [22] And the Lord heard the voice of Elijah; and the soul of the child came into him again, and he revived. [23] And Elijah took the child, and brought him down out of the chamber into the house, and delivered him unto his mother: and Elijah said, See, thy son liveth.

PROVERBS 16:18

Pride goeth before destruction, and an haughty spirit before a fall

1 KINGS 19:9-13

And he came thither unto a cave, and lodged there; and, behold, the word of the LORD came to him, and he said unto him, What doest thou here, Elijah? [10] And he said, I have been very jealous for the LORD God of hosts: for the children of Israel have forsaken thy covenant, thrown down thine altars, and slain thy prophets with the sword; and I, even I only, am left; and they seek my life, to take it away. [11] And he said, Go forth, and stand upon the mount before the LORD. And, behold, the LORD passed by, and a great and strong wind rent the mountains, and brake in pieces the rocks before the LORD; but the LORD was not in the wind: and after the wind an earthquake; but the LORD was not in the earthquake: [12] And after the earthquake a fire; but the LORD was not in the fire: and after the fire a still small voice. [13] And it was so, when Elijah heard it, that he wrapped his face in his mantle, and went out, and stood in the entering in of the cave. And, behold, there came a voice unto him, and said, What doest thou here, Elijah?

1 KINGS 18:13

Was it not told my lord what I did when Jezebel slew the prophets of the Lord, how I hid an hundred men of the Lord's prophets by fifty in a cave, and fed them with bread and water?

1 KINGS 19:15-16

And the LORD said unto him, Go, return on thy way to the wilderness of Damascus: and when thou comest, anoint Hazael to be king over Syria: [16] And Jehu the son of Nimshi shalt thou anoint to be king over Israel: and Elisha the son of Shaphat of Abelmeholah shalt thou anoint to be prophet in thy room.

1 KINGS 19:19-21

So he departed thence, and found Elisha the son of Shaphat, who was plowing with twelve yoke of oxen before him, and he with the twelfth: and Elijah passed by him, and cast his mantle upon him. [20] And he left the oxen, and ran after Elijah, and said, Let me, I pray thee, kiss my father and my mother, and then I will follow thee. And he said unto him, Go back again: for what have I done to thee? [21] And he returned back from him, and took a yoke of oxen, and slew them, and boiled their flesh with the instruments of the oxen, and gave unto the people, and they did eat. Then he arose, and went after Elijah, and ministered unto him.

2 KINGS 8:13

And Hazael said, But what, is thy servant a dog, that he should do this great thing? And Elisha answered, The LORD hath shewed me that thou shalt be king over Syria.

2 KINGS 9:1-6

And Elisha the prophet called one of the children of the prophets, and said unto him, Gird up thy loins, and take this box of oil in thine hand, and go to Ramothgilead: [2] And when thou comest thither, look out there Jehu the son of Jehoshaphat the son of Nimshi, and go in, and make him arise up from among his brethren, and carry him to an inner chamber; [3] Then take the box of oil, and pour it on his head, and say, Thus saith the LORD, I have anointed thee king over Israel. Then open the door, and flee, and tarry not. [4] So the young man, even the young man the prophet, went to Ramothgilead. [5] And when he came, behold, the captains of the host were sitting; and he said, I have an errand to thee, O captain. And Jehu said, Unto which of all us? And he said, To thee, O captain. [6] And he arose, and went into the house; and he poured the oil on his head, and said unto him, Thus saith the LORD God of Israel, I have anointed thee king over the people of the LORD, even over Israel.

2 KINGS 2:11

And it came to pass, as they still went on, and talked, that, behold, there appeared a chariot of fire, and horses of fire, and parted them both asunder; and Elijah went up by a whirlwind into heaven.

GENESIS 5:24

And Enoch walked with God: and he was not; for God took him.

ROMANS 5:20

Moreover the law entered, that the offence might abound. But where sin abounded, grace did much more abound.

GLORIFY THE LORD

LESSON 13.1

Because that which may be known of God is manifest in them; for God hath shewed it unto them. [20] For the invisible things of him from the creation of the world are clearly seen, being understood by the things that are made, even his eternal power and Godhead; so that they are without excuse.

ROMANS 1:19-20

In this verse, the Apostle Paul was explaining that we don't have to tell people how unholy they are—they already know it. We all possess an intuitive knowledge that God is holy and we are not. It's true that some people have hardened their hearts by repeatedly turning away from God. They may say they have no conviction about living in sin, but in truth, God has revealed Himself to every human being, and we all know in our hearts that sin is wrong.

The Bible says, *"Be still, and know that I am God"* (Ps. 46:10). The reason people always want the television or music on or are constantly doing something is because they don't want to be still. If you are still and quiet, this little homing device that God placed on the inside of you starts going off and asking, "Is this all there is to life?" Stillness brings an awareness of God; the world drowns this out with activity.

Our hearts speak to us twenty-four hours a day. Every minute of every day, God reveals Himself to us—but the noise of this world drowns out the still, small voice of God. We can deaden ourselves or get calloused to the voice of God, but God will never stop reaching out to us. We don't need someone to tell us that God exists. Every person on the planet, at one time or another, has known that God is real. After a while, we can become so accustomed to living out of our natural understanding that our hearts become hardened, and we don't remember ever knowing God. But really, everyone has known God is real from the time they were little.

It's just a mind game. In the Vietnam War, I saw people who claimed to be atheists cry out to God the minute bullets started flying and bombs began dropping. When crisis comes and the illusion of control is shattered, unbelievers cry out for God to save them because in their hearts, they know that He is real and that He can save them. I quit arguing with people about whether or not God exists. You can't argue a person into believing in God, because by claiming not to believe in God, they are choosing to ignore all of the evidence around them.

The Bible says the things of God are clearly seen. Anyone who says they don't believe God exists is either lying, or they have hardened their hearts to the truth. It's possible to push God far enough away or harden your heart to the extreme that you become a *"reprobate"*—this means that God takes all conviction away from you (Rom. 1:28). Nobody can come to the Father unless the Holy Spirit draws them (John 6:44), so you are damned if the Holy Spirit quits drawing you. Even at that point, though, it doesn't mean you don't know that God exists—it just means that you are past feeling remorse for rebelling against Him.

Nobody will ever be able to stand before God and claim that His judgment isn't fair because they never knew He existed. Every person who has ever drawn a breath on this planet has known there's a God. People can harden themselves to the point of rejecting God entirely, but it doesn't happen quickly. Generally, it takes time to become as numb to God as society is today. Insensitivity to God is built up by countless denials of the simple witness of God in your heart, but it happens.

Staying Sensitive to God

Because that, when they knew God, they glorified him not as God, neither were thankful; but became vain in their imaginations, and their foolish heart was darkened.

ROMANS 1:21

The steps in this passage describe the progressive process by which people's hearts can become hardened toward God. It shows the desensitization process that someone goes through. No one is going to fulfill God's will for their life by allowing their heart to become hardened toward Him. We need to avoid this downward spiral. I believe that if we do the opposite of the process described in this scripture, we will remain sensitive to God and avoid being desensitized.

This verse says that although they knew God, they didn't glorify Him as God. The Greek word used here for *"glorified"* means "to render (or esteem) glorious" (*Strong's Concordance*)—which is another way of saying to value, or to prize. In other words, they didn't value or prize the things of God. This is important because Satan will always try to get us to decrease the value, esteem, or worth that we place on the things of God. Unfortunately, the devil doesn't have to work very hard to entice most people down this path. We live in a carnal world, and the things of God are not valued by the world. When we share the values of the world instead of His values, the hardening process begins. The Lord's values are completely different from most of what the world values. The Apostle John put it this way:

> Love not the world, neither the things that are in the world. If any man love the world, the love of the Father is not in him. [16] For all that is in the world, the lust of the flesh, and the lust of the eyes, and the pride of life, is not of the Father, but is of the world.
>
> 1 JOHN 2:15-16

Christians watch the same junk on television that unbelievers watch. They read the same garbage and listen to the same ungodly music. The majority of Christians use the same things for entertainment as the world. Is it any wonder that the church is becoming more and more like the world? The world says that God is dead, He doesn't exist, and none of the miracles we see in the name of God are real. We can't share the world's values without becoming desensitized to God. *Whatever we focus our attention on is going to dominate us.* The Holy Spirit draws us toward a more intimate relationship with God, while the world pulls us the other way.

I have seen people raised from the dead. I have seen blind eyes opened. I have seen every type of miracle you can imagine, and people say to me, "If those miracles are real, then why don't you put it on the nightly news for everyone to see? Why don't you verify all of the miracles you see?" I don't bother, because there would be no point. The world doesn't believe in miracles. The world doesn't value the things of God, so they cannot accept that miracles are real. Unbelievers would sit in front of their televisions and try to find a way to deny the report, hardening their hearts even more. They would see someone get up out of a wheelchair, and say, "Well, she must not have been all that bad off to begin with."

Contrary to what some think—seeing is *not* believing. Neither does faith come by miracles. Faith comes by the Word of God (Rom. 10:17). Miracles help those who already believe or want to believe but are struggling with doubt. Miracles help us remove doubt, but faith only comes through the Word of God.

People gathered at the tomb of Lazarus and saw Jesus raise him from the dead. They watched it with their own eyes (John 11:38-45). Lazarus had been dead and buried for several days. His body was already decaying. When Jesus told them to roll away the gravestone, Lazarus' sister protested that there would be an odor because he had already been dead four days. Lazarus was wrapped head to toe in grave clothes; both of his legs were wrapped together like a mummy—he couldn't walk. This means that when Jesus called him to "come forth" (John 11:43), God supernaturally translated him to the opening of the cave.

Everyone standing there saw a corpse raised from the dead, but they didn't let it change what they believed. Some of them conspired to kill Jesus and Lazarus with Him (John 11:46-53). If you have a heart to disbelieve, you won't believe even if you see someone raised from the dead—which is exactly what Jesus taught in the parable of the rich man (Luke 16:19-31). Jesus said that if people won't believe Moses and the prophets—the Word of God—they won't believe a miracle either.

You can have a tremendous experience with the Lord on Sunday, but when you go to your place of work on Monday, Satan is going to parade people by you who will try to devalue your experience. Whenever you make a commitment to God or something miraculous happens, you are going to have family, friends, work associates, or somebody laugh at you when you tell them what happened. They aren't going to appreciate your experience to the degree that you do. This is one way that Satan tries to change the value you place on the things of God. It is similar to the way a seesaw works: When your opinion of God is up, everyone else's opinion is going to be lower or of less significance. On the other hand, if you start accepting the values and views of people, your esteem for the things of God will decrease. It isn't possible to highly value both the opinion of man and the opinion of God at the same time.

Jesus said, "How can you believe, which receive honor from one another, and seek not the honor that comes from God only?" (John 5:44). It is impossible to really believe God when you are a man-pleaser. Most people are dependent on the approval of others. They don't like being rejected or ridiculed, so they value the opinion of other people more than they value God's opinion. Proverbs says the fear of man brings a snare (Prov. 29:25). Nobody likes rejection, but you can't be troubled by it, because the first step to diminishing the impact of God in your life is to start worrying about what other people have to say.

The Bible says that all who live godly in Christ Jesus will suffer persecution (2 Tim. 3:12). You haven't been living a godly life for very long if you've never suffered persecution. If you never bump into the devil, it's because you and the devil are both heading in the same direction. When you turn around and start going against the flow, you are going to meet resistance. You will encounter persecution. If you are more concerned with the approval of people than you are with God, you will quit glorifying God. The moment you shift your value system to exalt the opinions of other people above God, your heart begins to harden.

A long time ago, as I was hiking up Pikes Peak with a friend of mine, he began to talk about a guy who was very critical of us—a guy who was supposedly our friend. Whenever we were around him, he was sweet and everything was fine. But behind our backs, he constantly criticized us. My friend and I had discussed this situation before because it really bothered him. So, as we were hiking up Pikes Peak, he started telling me the latest thing that this pastor was saying about us behind our backs.

I said, "I don't want to hear it. I know this guy doesn't like us, but I just don't care."

My friend started to say something in response, but then stopped. Finally, he said, "Why don't the things he is saying bother you like they bother me?"

I told him, "Because I don't value his opinion the way you do."

The only people who will ever let us down are the people we lean on. God will never let us down, so we need to lean on Him. It's not that we don't care about other people; it's just that we shouldn't need them to pat us on the back in order to feel good about ourselves. We need to bask in the fact that our heavenly Father loves us. Then, when criticism comes, even though we don't like it, it won't keep us up at night. When we esteem God's opinion the highest, what other people have to say just won't matter all that much.

I experienced God's love in a huge way on March 23, 1968, and it transformed my life. I stood up on Sunday morning and told the whole church how God had changed me. I didn't know how to describe what had happened, so I told them I was "filled with the Holy Spirit." Boy, they jumped on me like a chicken on a June bug! The pastor said to me, "Who do you think you are? The Apostle Paul was filled with the Spirit. Peter was filled with the Spirit. Are you saying you're like an apostle? Are you better than the rest of us?" I didn't mean anything by saying that I was filled with the Spirit; I was just trying to communicate what had happened to me. But the people around me tried to devalue what God had done.

I was glorifying God. I was celebrating what He had done—and immediately an authority figure came along and tried to get me to value his opinion above God's by asking, "Who do you think you are?" In his eyes, I was just an eighteen-year-old kid, whereas he was a pastor who had been to seminary. He wanted me to value his opinion more. The youth leader of the church, the pastor of the church, friends, relatives, and everybody else told me that I was missing God.

All of those things were an attempt to get me to put greater worth on the opinion of others than on God. If I had valued their opinion and started doubting what I felt in my heart, I would have quit glorifying God—and I would have taken the first step toward losing the fullness of joy and victory I had through my experience with the Lord. I didn't understand much back then, but by the grace of God, I just kept thinking, *I don't know what your problem is, but I know God has spoken to me.* I knew I had encountered God—all of the criticism that came rolled off me like water off a duck's back.

Shortly after I quit college, I became reclassified as "available for service" in the military draft system. Before I was drafted, a recruiter came to my house and explained the benefits of volunteering for service. He was dressed in his military uniform and did his best to project an authoritative presence. He sat down in my living room, spread out all of his pamphlets and started telling me how volunteering could keep me out of Vietnam. He was only partway into his spiel when I stopped him.

"Look," I said, "I can save us both a lot of time."

"Really, how's that?" he asked.

I began to tell him my story: "The reason that I was reclassified for the draft and you're here is because I quit school and lost my student deferment."

"That's right," he said.

"But, you see," I said, "God told me to quit school. So, I'm following God. And if God wants me to be drafted, then I'll be drafted, but if He doesn't, I won't."

The recruiter burst out in laughter. "Boy," he said, gasping for breath, "I can guarantee, you *are* going to Vietnam."

When he did that, something inside of me snapped. I was valuing God; His will was more important to me than anything else in my life. I believed God was all powerful. I was esteeming the things of God. Yet in front of me was an authority figure who placed zero worth on God. His attitude was, *I represent the United States government—who is God compared to me?*

When that attitude came across, anger rose up inside of me. I stood up, poked my finger into his chest, and said, "Buddy, if God wants me to get drafted, then I'll be drafted. And if He doesn't, you or the United States government or every demon in hell can't draft me." That might not have been the best way to handle it, but I was saying, "I value God and His opinion more than what you have to say."

The recruiter never said another word. He looked at me, folded up all of his papers, put them in his briefcase, and walked out the door. I received my draft notice in the mail the very next morning! I didn't think about it back then, but I should have looked to see if it even had a postmark or stamp on it. I bet that guy went back to his office, processed my papers himself, and then put the draft notice in my mailbox!

I don't know if that's the way it happened, and it doesn't matter, because I was trusting God. If I had started valuing the recruiter's opinion over God's, I would have started the process of hardening my heart. Before long, I would have felt like, *God, what happened to that experience where I knew how much You loved me and spoke to me and changed my life?*

In hindsight, Vietnam was the best thing that ever happened to me. I was religious when I went to Vietnam. For the thirteen months I was there, I studied the Word all day long. When I came back, I wasn't religious anymore. My theology had changed. I got hold of the grace of God and wasn't trying to fulfill religious duties to make myself worthy of God's love anymore. Vietnam was my Bible school; it was a good deal for me.

OUTLINE • 13.1

I. We all possess an intuitive knowledge that God is holy and we are not.

    Because that which may be known of God is manifest in them; for God hath shewed it unto them. [20] For the invisible things of him from the creation of the world are clearly seen, being understood by the things that are made, even his eternal power and Godhead; so that they are without excuse.

    ROMANS 1:19-20

    A. Some people may say they have no conviction about living in sin, but in truth, God has revealed Himself to every human being and we all know in our hearts that sin is wrong.

    B. The Bible says, *"Be still, and know that I am God"* (Ps. 46:10).

    C. Stillness brings an awareness of God; the world drowns this out with activity.

    D. Every minute of every day, God reveals Himself to us—but the noise of this world drowns out the still, small voice of God.

    E. We can deaden ourselves or get calloused to the voice of God, but God will never stop reaching out to us.

    F. It's possible to push God far enough away or harden our hearts to the extreme that we become *"reprobate"*—this means that God takes all conviction away from us (Rom. 1:28).

    G. Even at that point, though, it doesn't mean we don't know that God exists—it just means that we are past feeling remorse for rebelling against Him.

    H. Insensitivity to God is built up by countless denials of the simple witness of God in our hearts, but it happens.

II. The steps in this passage describe the progressive process by which people's hearts can become hardened toward God:

    Because that, when they knew God, they glorified him not as God, neither were thankful; but became vain in their imaginations, and their foolish heart was darkened.

    ROMANS 1:21

    A. No one is going to fulfill God's will for their life by allowing their heart to become hardened toward Him.

    B. I believe that if we do the opposite of the process described in this scripture, we will remain sensitive to God and avoid being desensitized.

    C. This verse says that although they knew God, they didn't glorify Him as God.

D. The Greek word used here for *"glorified"* means "to render (or esteem) glorious" (*Strong's Concordance*)—which is another way of saying to value, or to prize.

E. In other words, they didn't value or prize the things of God.

F. This is important because Satan will always try to get us to decrease the value, esteem, or worth that we place on the things of God.

G. When we share the values of the carnal world instead of His values, the hardening process begins.

H. The Lord's values are completely different from most of what the world values.

Love not the world, neither the things that are in the world. If any man love the world, the love of the Father is not in him. [16] For all that is in the world, the lust of the flesh, and the lust of the eyes, and the pride of life, is not of the Father, but is of the world.

1 JOHN 2:15-16

I. *Whatever we focus our attention on is going to dominate us*—the Holy Spirit draws us toward a more intimate relationship with God, while the world pulls us the other way.

J. When our opinion of God is up, everyone else's opinion is going to be lower or of less significance.

K. On the other hand, if we start accepting the values and views of people, our esteem for the things of God will decrease.

L. It isn't possible to highly value both the opinion of man and the opinion of God at the same time (John 5:44 and Prov. 29:25).

M. Nobody likes rejection, but we can't be troubled by it, because the first step to diminishing the impact of God in our lives is to start worrying about what other people have to say (2 Tim. 3:12).

N. It's not that we don't care about other people; it's just that we shouldn't need them to pat us on the back in order to feel good about ourselves.

O. When we esteem God's opinion the highest, what other people have to say just won't matter all that much.

1. We all possess an intuitive knowledge that God is holy and we are not.

> *Because that which may be known of God is manifest in them; for God hath shewed it unto them. [20] For the invisible things of him from the creation of the world are clearly seen, being understood by the things that are made, even his eternal power and Godhead; so that they are without excuse.*
> ROMANS 1:19-20

Some people may say they have no conviction about living in sin, but in truth, God has revealed Himself to every human being and we all know in our hearts that sin is wrong. The Bible says, *"Be still, and know that I am God"* (Ps. 46:10). Stillness brings an awareness of God; the world drowns this out with activity. Every minute of every day, God reveals Himself to us—but the noise of this world drowns out the still, small voice of God. We can deaden ourselves or get calloused to the voice of God, but God will never stop reaching out to us. It's possible to push God far enough away or harden our hearts to the extreme that we become *"reprobate"*—this means that God takes all conviction away from us (Rom. 1:28). Even at that point, though, it doesn't mean we don't know that God exists—it just means that we are past feeling remorse for rebelling against Him. Insensitivity to God is built up by countless denials of the simple witness of God in our hearts, but it happens.

1a. Romans 1:19-20 says, *"Because that which may be known of God is _____ in them; for God hath shewed it unto them. [20] For the invisible things of him from the creation of the world are _____ seen, being understood by the things that are made, even his eternal power and Godhead; so that they are without _____."* **_"Manifest" / "clearly" / "excuse"_**

1b. Discussion question: Why do you think people deny God and ignore the conviction about their sin? Have you ever experienced a situation similar to this? How did you resolve it? **_Discussion question_**

1c. Which verse says to *"be still, and know that I am God"*? **Psalm 46:10**

1d. Discussion question: Do you think you need more stillness in your life? Why or why not? **_Discussion question_**

1e. True or false: It's possible to push God far enough away or harden your heart to the extreme that you become *"reprobate"* (Rom. 1:28). **True**

1f. _____ to God is built up by countless denials of the simple witness of God in your heart.
    A. Surrender
    B. Insensitivity
    C. Glory
    D. All of the above
    E. None of the above
    B. Insensitivity

2. The steps in this passage describe the progressive process by which people's hearts can become hardened toward God:

> *Because that, when they knew God, they glorified him not as God, neither were thankful; but became vain in their imaginations, and their foolish heart was darkened.*
>
> ROMANS 1:21

describe the progressive process by which people's hearts can become hardened toward God. No one is going to fulfill God's will for their life by allowing their heart to become hardened toward Him. I believe that if we do the opposite of the process described in this scripture, we will remain sensitive to God and avoid being desensitized. This verse says that although they knew God, they didn't glorify Him as God. The Greek word used here for *"glorified"* means "to render (or esteem) glorious" (*Strong's Concordance*)—which is another way of saying to value, or to prize. In other words, they didn't value or prize the things of God. This is important because Satan will always try to get us to decrease the value, esteem, or worth that we place on the things of God. When we share the values of the carnal world instead of His values, the hardening process begins. The Lord's values are completely different from most of what the world values.

> *Love not the world, neither the things that are in the world. If any man love the world, the love of the Father is not in him. [16] For all that is in the world, the lust of the flesh, and the lust of the eyes, and the pride of life, is not of the Father, but is of the world.*
>
> 1 JOHN 2:15-16

Whatever we focus our attention on is going to dominate us—the Holy Spirit draws us toward a more intimate relationship with God, while the world pulls us the other way. When our opinion of God is up, everyone else's opinion is going to be lower or of less significance. On the other hand, if we start accepting the values and views of people, our esteem for the things of God will decrease. It isn't possible to highly value both the opinion of man and the opinion of God at the same time (John 5:44 and Prov. 29:25). Nobody likes rejection, but we can't be troubled by it, because the first step to diminishing the impact of God in our lives is to start worrying about what other people have to say (2 Tim. 3:12). It's not that we don't care about other people; it's just that we shouldn't need them to pat us on the back in order to feel good about ourselves. When we esteem God's opinion the highest, what other people have to say just won't matter all that much.

2a. According to Romans 1:21, what are the steps described by which people's hearts can become hardened toward God?
"They glorified him not as God, neither were thankful; but became vain in their imaginations, and their foolish heart was darkened"

2b. Discussion question: Why do you think a hardened heart will keep you from fulfilling God's will?
Discussion question

2c. What will happen if you do the opposite of what's described in Romans 1:21?
You will remain sensitive to God and avoid being desensitized

2d. Satan will always try to get us to decrease the _____, _____, or _____ that we place on the things of God.
Value / esteem / worth

2e. Discussion question: This lesson says that the Lord's values are completely different from most of what the world values. Where do you feel your values lay—closer to the Lord's values or closer to the world's? What, if anything, do you think should change?
Discussion question

2f. Discussion question: What are your thoughts on the idea that "whatever we focus our attention on is going to dominate us?"
Discussion question

2g. True or false: The first step to diminishing the impact of God in your life is to start ignoring what other people have to say.
False

DISCIPLESHIP QUESTIONS • 13.1

1. Romans 1:19-20 says, *"Because that which may be known of God is _____ in them; for God hath shewed it unto them. [20] For the invisible things of him from the creation of the world are _____ seen, being understood by the things that are made, even his eternal power and Godhead; so that they are without _____."*

2. Discussion question: Why do you think people deny God and ignore the conviction about their sin? Have you ever experienced a situation similar to this? How did you resolve it?

   _____

   _____

   _____

3. Which verse says to *"be still, and know that I am God"*?

   _____

   _____

   _____

4. Discussion question: Do you think you need more stillness in your life? Why or why not?

   _____

   _____

   _____

5. True or false: It's possible to push God far enough away or harden your heart to the extreme that you become *"reprobate"* (Rom. 1:28).

6. _____ to God is built up by countless denials of the simple witness of God in your heart.
   A. Surrender
   B. Insensitivity
   C. Glory
   D. All of the above
   E. None of the above

7. According to Romans 1:21, what are the steps described by which man's hearts can become hardened toward God?

_____

_____

_____

8. Discussion question: Why do you think a hardened heart will keep you from fulfilling God's will?

_____

_____

_____

9. What will happen if you do the opposite of what's described in Romans 1:21?

_____

_____

_____

10. Satan will always try to get us to decrease the _____, _____, or _____ that we place on the things of God.

11. Discussion question: This lesson says that the Lord's values are completely different from most of what the world values. Where do you feel your values lay—closer to the Lord's values or closer to the world's? What, if anything, do you think should change?

_____

_____

_____

12. Discussion question: What are your thoughts on the idea that "whatever we focus our attention on is going to dominate us?"

_____

_____

_____

13. True or false: The first step to diminishing the impact of God in your life is to start ignoring what other people have to say.

_____

_____

_____

ANSWER KEY • 13.1

1. *"Manifest" / "clearly" / "excuse"*
2. *Discussion question*
3. Psalm 46:10
4. *Discussion question*
5. True
6. B. Insensitivity
7. *"They glorified him not as God, neither were thankful; but became vain in their imaginations, and their foolish heart was darkened"*
8. *Discussion question*
9. You will remain sensitive to God and avoid being desensitized
10. Value / esteem / worth
11. *Discussion question*
12. *Discussion question*
13. False

ROMANS 1:19-21

Because that which may be known of God is manifest in them; for God hath shewed it unto them. [20] For the invisible things of him from the creation of the world are clearly seen, being understood by the things that are made, even his eternal power and Godhead; so that they are without excuse: [21] Because that, when they knew God, they glorified him not as God, neither were thankful; but became vain in their imaginations, and their foolish heart was darkened.

PSALM 46:10

Be still, and know that I am God: I will be exalted among the heathen, I will be exalted in the earth.

ROMANS 1:28

And even as they did not like to retain God in their knowledge, God gave them over to a reprobate mind, to do those things which are not convenient.

JOHN 6:44

No man can come to me, except the Father which hath sent me draw him: and I will raise him up at the last day.

1 JOHN 2:15-16

Love not the world, neither the things that are in the world. If any man love the world, the love of the Father is not in him. [16] For all that is in the world, the lust of the flesh, and the lust of the eyes, and the pride of life, is not of the Father, but is of the world.

ROMANS 10:17

So then faith cometh by hearing, and hearing by the word of God.

JOHN 11:38-53

Jesus therefore again groaning in himself cometh to the grave. It was a cave, and a stone lay upon it. [39] Jesus said, Take ye away the stone. Martha, the sister of him that was dead, saith unto him, Lord, by this time he stinketh: for he hath been dead four days. [40] Jesus saith unto her, Said I not unto thee, that, if thou wouldest believe, thou shouldest see the glory of God? [41] Then they took away the stone from the place where the dead was laid. And Jesus lifted up his eyes, and said, Father, I thank thee that thou hast heard me. [42] And I knew that thou hearest me always: but because of the people which stand by I said it, that they may believe that thou hast sent me. [43] And when he thus had spoken, he cried with a loud voice, Lazarus, come forth. [44] And he that was dead came forth, bound hand and foot with graveclothes: and his face was bound about with a napkin. Jesus saith unto them, Loose him, and let him go. [45] Then many of the Jews which came to Mary, and had seen the things which Jesus did, believed on him. [46] But some of them went their ways to the Pharisees, and told them what things Jesus had done. [47] Then gathered the chief priests and the Pharisees a council, and said, What do we? for this man doeth many miracles. [48] If we let him thus alone, all men will believe on him: and the Romans shall come and take away both our place and nation. [49] And one of them, named Caiaphas, being the high priest that same year, said unto them, Ye know nothing at all, [50] Nor consider that it is expedient for us, that one man should die for the people, and that the whole nation perish not. [51] And this spake he not of himself: but being high priest that year, he prophesied that Jesus should die for that nation; [52] And not for that nation only, but that also he should gather together in one the children of God that were scattered abroad. [53] Then from that day forth they took counsel together for to put him to death.

LUKE 16:19-31

There was a certain rich man, which was clothed in purple and fine linen, and fared sumptuously every day: [20] And there was a certain beggar named Lazarus, which was laid at his gate, full of sores, [21] And desiring to be fed with the crumbs which fell from the rich man's table: moreover the dogs came and licked his sores. [22] And it came to pass, that the beggar died, and was carried by the angels into Abraham's bosom: the rich man also died, and was buried; [23] And in hell he lift up his eyes, being in torments, and seeth Abraham afar off, and Lazarus in his bosom. [24] And he cried and said, Father Abraham, have mercy on me, and send Lazarus, that he may dip the tip of his finger in water, and cool my tongue; for I am tormented in this flame. [25] But Abraham said, Son, remember that thou in thy lifetime receivedst thy good things, and likewise Lazarus evil things: but now he is comforted, and thou art tormented. [26] And beside all this, between us and you there is a great gulf fixed: so that they which would pass from hence to you cannot; neither can they pass to us, that would come from thence. [27] Then he said, I pray thee therefore, father, that thou wouldest send him to my father's house: [28] For I have five brethren; that he may testify unto them, lest they also come into this place of torment. [29] Abraham saith unto him, They have Moses and the prophets; let them hear them. [30] And he said, Nay, father Abraham: but if one went unto them from the dead, they will repent. [31] And he said unto him, If they hear not Moses and the prophets, neither will they be persuaded, though one rose from the dead.

JOHN 5:44

How can ye believe, which receive honour one of another, and seek not the honour that cometh from God only?

PROVERBS 29:25

The fear of man bringeth a snare: but whoso putteth his trust in the LORD shall be safe.

2 TIMOTHY 3:12

Yea, and all that will live godly in Christ Jesus shall suffer persecution.

LESSON 13.2

The flow of God's love can only be stopped by us. When we run into a dry spell, it isn't because God shut off the spigot. God speaks His love to us twenty-four hours a day, seven days a week. One of the most common prayer requests I get is from people who want God to reveal His love to them. Their hearts are right in desiring to know God's love, but ignorance of God's love isn't the result of Him holding something back. God is constantly showering us with His love, so if we don't know the love of God, it's because we aren't receiving what He has already given us. God loves us; no prayer is going to motivate Him to love us more.

A woman once told me how she had been praying twenty years for her husband to be saved. She told me that God didn't answer her prayer, but she believed He would answer mine. So, she asked me to pray for God to save her husband. The way she phrased it made it sound like she thought it was up to God whether or not her husband received salvation. I told her, "God has already done everything about saving your husband He can do. He already sent His Son. He died. The Holy Spirit is working in you to help him get saved. You think that somehow or another, God isn't motivated to save your husband, but He is more motivated for your husband to be saved than you are. You don't need to beg God to save your husband; your husband needs to hear the Gospel and believe."

Faith comes by hearing and hearing by the Word of God, so I told her to pray for laborers to come across her husband's path to tell him about the Gospel. I told her to tell him the Good News herself, to love him, and to be a good example. Those are the things we can do to help someone get saved; we don't have to encourage God to save anybody. God is far more motivated about salvation than we are.

Sometimes when people receive the baptism of the Holy Spirit at one of my meetings, they have an ecstatic experience, get overwhelmed, and start speaking in tongues loudly, as if they can't control it. The baptism of the Holy Spirit is a good thing to get excited about, but

I always stop them for a moment to show them that they don't have to feel ecstatic in order to pray in tongues. They won't always get goose bumps and have chills. It's great to feel those things, but they don't need to be emotionally overwhelmed to speak in tongues. They can pray in tongues whether they feel anything or not.

Someone might ask, "Are you saying that I can just turn the Holy Ghost on and off?" No, the Holy Ghost is *on* all of the time! People turn themselves on and off, but the Holy Spirit is always on. All we need to do is speak in tongues to turn ourselves back on. The Bible tells us to build ourselves up in our holy faith by praying in the Holy Ghost, and to keep ourselves in the love of God (Jude 20-21). It's up to us whether or not we feel the love of God. It's up to us whether we are happy and joyful. It's not up to God.

God has placed His love, joy, and peace on the inside of us. Whenever we aren't feeling the love of God, it's because we have begun to value something else—diminishing what God has spoken to us. We can even lose our joy by esteeming our own efforts to please God, instead of esteeming God's grace and the finished work of Jesus. So, we shouldn't pray for God to give us joy again; let's just go back to valuing God and believing His Word.

Another way to explain what it means to glorify the Lord is to use the word *magnify*. The same Greek word that was translated *"glorified"* in Romans 1:21 was translated *"magnify"* in Romans 11:13. So, when we place value on God and focus on what He has done, it magnifies Him. Technically speaking, God is who He is, regardless of what we think. Ignoring God doesn't make Him smaller, just as failing to value or glorify Him doesn't change how big He is—but it will change our perception.

We may not relate to God in a way that magnifies Him, but it's *our* value that gets altered, not His. The way we magnify God in our own lives is by placing value on Him and recognizing the things He is doing in our lives and the words He has spoken to us. *Focusing on God makes Him get bigger in our way of thinking and perceiving*. It makes Him bigger than sickness and tragedy. Magnifying God takes us to a place where we don't fall apart like a two-dollar suitcase every time something bad happens. Esteeming God above all circumstances will make Him big and everything else small. It not only changes our outlook; it changes our experience of life.

Your mind is like a set of binoculars: Whatever you focus your attention on gets larger. It grows bigger and bigger, and the more you think about it, the bigger it gets. The stuff that most people get upset about is insignificant relative to eternity. Most of the things people worry about won't make any difference a million years from now. In eternity, you will look back and think, *What was I so worried about?*

Even though it's not a big deal, we make it a big deal. If the devil puts a little toothpick in our path, we magnify it, focus on it, and think about it until it becomes a huge obstacle in our mind. Then we begin to believe the little splinter is a giant redwood that we can't overcome, when in reality, the devil is just beating our brains out with a toothpick!

Sometimes, when people come to me with tears in their eyes and tell me what their problems are, I literally have to bite my lip to keep from laughing. I can't help thinking, *Is that all? This is what you're all upset over? I have worse things happen to me before I get out of bed in the morning.* But it's a big problem to them because they have magnified it. We need to do the exact opposite. We need to magnify God and focus on what He has done, until our problems shrink in comparison.

There were eight or nine people with me in the prayer meeting that changed my life on March 23, 1968. Every one of us was impacted by God. We all knew that God had been in that room, and we were all overwhelmed by His presence. My best friend was there, so the next morning, we talked about what had happened and said we would never be the same.

Today I am the only person who was in that room who still believes anything significant happened that night. Even though we all experienced the same thing, life, time, and adversity have talked them all out of the experience we shared. I'm the only one who still remembers what God did that night. As a matter of fact, my best friend, who received the baptism of the Holy Spirit and spoke in tongues, renounces speaking in tongues today.

Another good friend of mine who was there that night went through some terrible times that forced him out of the ministry. He wound up having an affair, and his life crashed. We parted ways a long time before any of that happened; but our friendship has been restored, and I've asked him about some of the things we experienced together. I asked him if he remembered a time God spoke to us or when we witnessed a manifestation of God's presence or any of the other things we experienced. But he didn't remember anything; he couldn't recall any of it.

The reason he couldn't remember the things God had done in his life was because he was very sensitive to people's opinions; he valued the opinions of man more than he valued God's opinion. He esteemed the approval of people above God, to the point that over forty years later, he couldn't even remember things that are as fresh to me as if they had happened yesterday. This proves that whatever you focus on gets bigger, while everything else gets smaller by contrast. If you focus on the approval of people and the values of this world, the things of God will shrink in comparison. But if you magnify God, the opinions of people and your problems will shrink.

Very few days go by that I don't thank God for what He has done for me. I am constantly saying, "Thank You, Father, for touching my life, and thank You for revealing Yourself to me." I glorify God and thank Him all the time. On the other hand, I have received a lot of criticism for preaching the Gospel. I have heard of people writing blogs against me on the internet. Some of them claim that I am "the most dangerous man in America."

People say terrible things about me. I could get into self-pity and magnify the bad things that are being said, but I prefer to glorify the Lord—not my problems. I respond by saying, "Father, I don't know what their problem is, but I know You love me. Thank You for touching my life." Because I have glorified God and put value on what He has done in my life, the events of March 23, 1968, are more powerful to me today than they were over forty years ago. I have never lost the joy of experiencing God's love for me.

God isn't responsible for turning off the flow of His power and love in our lives. Things can happen that make us lose sight of that truth—times of struggle that wear us down and leave us feeling a lack of joy—but I have learned what to do when I start losing my joy. I immediately change my focus and begin to glorify God. As I do this, everything falls into proper perspective and my joy returns.

Problems happen in life. Businesses fail, people say hurtful things, and loved ones die— but magnifying these problems only makes them seem even more tragic than they really are, causing your esteem of God to shrink. In order to make God bigger in your mind than your problems, you need to change your focus.

Go back and remember the joy and peace you experienced when you were first saved. Begin to thank God for filling you with the Holy Spirit and placing the same power inside of you that raised Christ from the dead. Recall the times that God has touched you or healed you. As you glorify God and value what He has done in your life, all of the other incidents that have robbed your joy and peace will fade away. You don't have to ask God for a fresh touch. You can turn to Him and refresh yourself anytime you want to be recharged.

I don't know if you listen to Christian music—or what is labeled as Christian music—but most of it is *ungodly* to the max. It's basically a Christian version of country and western music. Instead of complaining about losing your truck or your job, it whines about losing the presence of God. "O God, touch me again—I'm desperate for You. I've lost Your presence. Where did You go?" Some of the songs I hear are pathetic. Not all Christian music, but a lot of it, is just whining, griping, and complaining to God. That's the reason I love Charlie and Jill LeBlanc's music. They sing lyrics like, "My favorite thing to do is to spend my time with You," and they glorify God instead of whining about what's going on. *All whining does is verify, establish, and cement you into the problem you're in.*

I admit that a lot of people go through mountaintops and valleys in their relationship with God, but it isn't because God wants it that way. You can keep yourself as happy as you want to be. If you aren't thrilled with Him, it's not His fault. God hasn't failed you. You lose your joy when you quit glorifying Him and start focusing on your problems. Magnifying your problems can be as subtle as telling someone all about your hurts and pains when they ask, "How are you?" or rehearsing in your mind the wrong someone has done to you—mulling over it again and again until what was insignificant becomes a major concern.

I realize that not everyone wants to hear this. They say, "So, you're saying it's my fault?" Yes, that's exactly what I'm saying—but don't get upset or feel condemned. This is great news because it means you can do something to change your experience. If God ordained you to go through mountaintops and valleys and only enjoy His presence for an hour before it wears off, then you would just have to deal with it. You can't do anything to change God. Discovering that the problem is with *you* is cause for celebration because you can fix yourself. You can change the way you think. You can do something about your behavior.

Stop focusing on your problems and begin to glorify God. Rehearse your victories and talk about how good God is. As you magnify God, all of your problems will shrink down to nothing. Sickness, disease, worry, hurt, grief, and pain will fade away as you focus on how good God is. Glorifying God and being thankful are how you can stay in God's will. They will keep you from getting discouraged and giving up.

In the forty-plus years that I have been seeking God, this principle has been one of the most important factors in keeping what God has done in my life fresh. I have never gotten over what God has done for me—and I never will! I don't go a single day without thanking God for touching me and for the privilege of working in the ministry.

If I was God, I would have picked somebody more talented. I would have picked somebody better looking and who had a better voice. But I am so grateful that God chose me. I thank Him every day of my life for what He has done; therefore, I'm as happy and excited about God as I was all those years ago. Plus, now I have a lot more wisdom and experience. I wouldn't go back.

How many people, for one reason or another, talk about the "good ol' days"? I'm saying this with love, but if your days aren't good, it's your fault. This might be different from the way a lot of people think, but that doesn't mean it's wrong. These principles are scriptural. I'm giving my testimony that glorifying God instead of my problems has changed my life. It's working for me, and I've seen it work for others.

If the way you are living isn't producing the desired results, don't be resistant to change. If you are happy sometimes but depressed other times, why hang on to the beliefs that are causing your "up-and-down" experiences? Focusing on God and valuing Him in my life has kept me from getting depressed—and I've had a lot of depressing things happen.

We take for granted the incredible reality that God has sent His Spirit to indwell us. We have received the same Holy Spirit that created the heavens and the earth. We have a lot to praise God for. We need to recognize that we are the ones who shut off the flow of God's love. God never turns off His supply; we turn it off when we esteem and glorify something other than Him. In order to stay on track and finish our course, we have to keep the things of God fresh in our lives. And the primary way to stay sensitive to God is to glorify Him above everything else.

III. The flow of God's love can only be stopped by you.

    A. God is constantly showering you with His love, so if you don't know the love of God, it's because you aren't receiving what He has already given you.

    B. It's up to you whether or not you feel the love of God; it's up to you whether you are happy and joyful—it's not up to God.

    C. Whenever you aren't feeling the love of God, it's because you have begun to value something else—diminishing what God has spoken to you.

        i. You can even lose your joy by esteeming your own efforts to please God, instead of esteeming God's grace and the finished work of Jesus.

    D. Another way to explain what it means to glorify the Lord is to use the word *magnify*.

        i. The same Greek word that was translated *"glorified"* in Romans 1:21 was translated *"magnify"* in Romans 11:13.

    E. So, when you place value on God and focus on what He has done, it magnifies Him.

    F. Ignoring God doesn't make Him smaller, just as failing to value or glorify Him doesn't change how big He is—but it will change your perception.

    G. *Focusing on God makes Him get bigger in your way of thinking and perceiving.*

    H. Your mind is like a set of binoculars: Whatever you focus your attention on gets larger—it grows bigger and bigger, and the more you think about it, the bigger it gets.

    I. You need to do the exact opposite: You need to magnify God and focus on what He has done, until your problems shrink in comparison.

    J. A lot of people go through mountaintops and valleys in their relationship with God, but it isn't because God wants it that way.

    K. If God ordained you to go through mountaintops and valleys and only enjoy His presence for an hour before it wears off, then you would just have to deal with it—you can't do anything to change God.

    L. Discovering that the problem is with *you* is cause for celebration, because you can fix yourself—you can change the way you think; you can do something about your behavior.

    M. Stop focusing on your problems and begin to glorify God; rehearse your victories and talk about how good God is.

    N. Sickness, disease, worry, hurt, grief, and pain will fade away as you focus on how good God is.

    O. Glorifying God and being thankful are how you can stay in God's will—they will keep you from getting discouraged and giving up.

P. If the way you are living isn't producing the desired results, don't be resistant to change.

Q. In order to stay on track and finish your course, you have to keep the things of God fresh in your lives, and the primary way to stay sensitive to God is to glorify Him above everything else.

3. The flow of God's love can only be stopped by you. God is constantly showering you with His love, so if you don't know the love of God, it's because you aren't receiving what He has already given you. It's up to you whether or not you feel the love of God; it's up to you whether you are happy and joyful—it's not up to God. Whenever you aren't feeling the love of God, it's because you have begun to value something else—diminishing what God has spoken to you. You can even lose your joy by esteeming your own efforts to please God, instead of esteeming God's grace and the finished work of Jesus. Another way to explain what it means to glorify the Lord is to use the word *magnify*. The same Greek word that was translated *"glorified"* in Romans 1:21 was translated *"magnify"* in Romans 11:13. So, when you place value on God and focus on what He has done, it magnifies Him. Ignoring God doesn't make Him smaller, just as failing to value or glorify God doesn't change how big He is—but it will change your perception. *Focusing on God makes Him get bigger in your way of thinking and perceiving.* Your mind is like a set of binoculars: Whatever you focus your attention on gets larger—it grows bigger and bigger, and the more you think about it, the bigger it gets. You need to do the exact opposite: You need to magnify God and focus on what He has done, until your problems shrink in comparison. A lot of people go through mountaintops and valleys in their relationship with God, but it isn't because God wants it that way. If God ordained you to go through mountaintops and valleys and only enjoy His presence for an hour before it wears off, then you would just have to deal with it—you can't do anything to change God. Discovering that the problem is with *you* is cause for celebration, because you can fix yourself—you can change the way you think; you can do something about your behavior. Stop focusing on your problems and begin to glorify God; rehearse your victories and talk about how good God is. Sickness, disease, worry, hurt, grief, and pain will fade away as you focus on how good God is. Glorifying God and being thankful are how you can stay in God's will—they will keep you from getting discouraged and giving up. If the way you are living isn't producing the desired results, don't be resistant to change. In order to stay on track and finish your course, you have to keep the things of God fresh in your lives, and the primary way to stay sensitive to God is to glorify Him above everything else.

3a. Who is the only one who can stop the flow of God's love?
   A. You
   B. Satan
   C. Your pastor
   D. All of the above
   E. None of the above
   A. You

3b. What is not up to God?
   A. Whether or not you feel the love of God
   B. Whether you are happy and joyful
   C. If you have begun to value something else
   D. All of the above
   E. None of the above
   D. All of the above

3c. What happens when you place value on God and focus on what He has done?
It magnifies Him

3d. Discussion question: What are some examples of situations where focusing on God and making Him bigger in your way of thinking and perceiving have helped you overcome difficulties? (If you are unable to give examples from your own life, cite examples from the Bible.)
Discussion question

3e. Discussion question: Have you experienced focusing on something, positive or negative, until the more you thought about it, the bigger it got? How did this help/hinder you?
Discussion question

3f. Why is discovering that the problem is with you a cause for celebration?
Because you can fix yourself—you can change the way you think; you can do something about your behavior

3g. Discussion question: What are some of the victories you've had in God and some of the ways He has been good to you?
Discussion question

3h. Are glorifying God and being thankful how you can stay in God's will?
Yes

14. Who is the only one who can stop the flow of God's love?
    A. You
    B. Satan
    C. Your pastor
    D. All of the above
    E. None of the above

15. What is not up to God?
    A. Whether or not you feel the love of God
    B. Whether you are happy and joyful
    C. If you have begun to value something else
    D. All of the above
    E. None of the above

16. What happens when you place value on God and focus on what He has done?

    _____

    _____

    _____

17. Discussion question: What are some examples of situations where focusing on God and making Him bigger in your way of thinking and perceiving have helped you overcome difficulties? (If you are unable to give examples from your own life, cite examples from the Bible.)

    _____

    _____

    _____

18. Discussion question: Have you experienced focusing on something, positive or negative, until the more you thought about it, the bigger it got? How did this help/hinder you?

    _____

    _____

    _____

19. Why is discovering that the problem is with you a cause for celebration?

_____

_____

_____

20. Discussion question: What are some of the victories you've had in God and some of the ways He has been good to you?

_____

_____

_____

21. Are glorifying God and being thankful how you can stay in God's will?

_____

_____

_____

14. A. You
15. D. All of the above
16. It magnifies Him
17. *Discussion question*
18. *Discussion question*
19. Because you can fix yourself—you can change the way you think; you can do something about your behavior
20. *Discussion question*
21. Yes

JUDE 1:20-21
But ye, beloved, building up yourselves on your most holy faith, praying in the Holy Ghost, [21] Keep yourselves in the love of God, looking for the mercy of our Lord Jesus Christ unto eternal life.

ROMANS 1:21
Because that, when they knew God, they glorified him not as God, neither were thankful; but became vain in their imaginations, and their foolish heart was darkened.

ROMANS 11:13
For I speak to you Gentiles, inasmuch as I am the apostle of the Gentiles, I magnify mine office.

THANKFULNESS WILL
TAKE YOU PLACES

LESSON 14.1

Because that, when they knew God, they glorified him not as God, neither were thankful; but became vain in their imaginations, and their foolish heart was darkened.

ROMANS 1:21

As I pointed out in the last lesson, this scripture describes the steps that people take to deaden themselves to God. I'm turning these steps around to illustrate how we can stay sensitive to God and keep ourselves on track. Instead of failing to glorify God, being unthankful, and having a vain imagination, we want to glorify God, be thankful, and have a godly imagination. These few things will help keep us sensitive to God and fulfill our purpose.

We don't have to lose the joy in our relationship with God. In fact, our relationship with God should be getting better over time. Believers should be getting stronger and stronger in the Lord as time goes on. God never intended for the potency of our relationship with Him to fade, yet that is exactly what happens to many Christians. God touched them at some point, but the vibrancy of their experience faded. People tell me all the time how they had a powerful encounter with God at one of my meetings, but often, they lose their excitement about the Lord once they get back home. It shouldn't be that way.

In the last lesson, I covered how the first step in staying sensitive to God and maintaining the intensity of our relationship with Him is to glorify Him—to value His opinion above the opinions of man. But the factors listed here in Romans all work together; they are a package. For the purpose of discussion, though, I have separated them into different topics. This is really a description of a singular lifestyle on how to seek God and put Him first in your life. In terms of practical living, however, glorifying God, being thankful, and having a godly imagination aren't separate issues; they are all interconnected. So, this second step of thankfulness is something we add to our lifestyle of glorifying God in all circumstances.

I will praise the name of God with a song, and will magnify him with thanksgiving.
PSALM 69:30

Jesus quoted several passages from this psalm when He was dying on the cross. This prophetic psalm was written by David hundreds of years before Jesus came to earth, but by the power of the Holy Spirit, this is Jesus speaking. He says that He will magnify God with thanksgiving. The way you make God look bigger than sickness, poverty, rejection, or any other problem is by thanking Him. Being thankful and rehearsing your victories makes God bigger in your perspective. It puts more glory, worth, and value on Him.

This is a *powerful*, powerful truth. Christians ought to be thankful people. We should rehearse our victories on a regular basis. In fact, this is the reason there are a number of scriptures in the Old Testament that commanded the Israelites not to take away their neighbor's landmark (Deut. 19:14, 27:17; Prov. 22:28, and 23:10). Landmarks served as a reminder. For example, Samuel raised a stone and called it Ebenezer—which means *"the* Lord *helped us"*—because they won a great victory in battle (1 Sam. 7:12). Every time people passed by this landmark, it reminded them of the victory God won for them over the Amalekites. In the same way, we need to erect landmarks in our lives to remind us of the victories God has won for us.

One month before we taped the first show of our television program, I was working on a trail at my house and did something *really* stupid. I was trying to maneuver a huge boulder around, and it ended up rolling over my head. I fell down and a 1,000-pound boulder rolled over my arm and bounced off my head. It should have killed me! The pain hit me immediately, and I jumped straight up off the ground and ran a quarter of a mile, screaming and praising God, before I even stopped to assess the damage. I wasn't sure my arm would still be there. God supernaturally protected me, though, and the only damage I suffered was a swollen hand. (By the way, when I told Jamie that the boulder bounced off my head, she laughed and said, "Of course.")

As a memorial of what God did for me that day, I put a sign in front of the boulder that says "The Lord saved my life March 23, 1999, when this boulder rolled over my head, arm, and hand," and then I wrote the scripture, *"The* Lord *preserves the simple"* (Ps. 116:6a). What I did was dumb. But God preserved me. Every time I walk by that boulder, the sign reminds me of how God saved my life.

I erected another landmark on the face of a flat rock at the start of a trail on my property. It says, "If you don't, I will." It's a reference to when Jesus entered Jerusalem, and He told the Pharisees that if the people didn't praise Him, the rocks would immediately cry out (Luke

19:40). So, every time I walk by that rock, I tell it to be quiet, and I start praising God and thanking Him for all He has done in my life.

> Bless the LORD, O my soul: and all that is within me, bless his holy name. *[2]*
> Bless the LORD, O my soul, and forget not all his benefits.
>
> PSALM 103:1-2

The reason this scripture tells us not to forget is because the natural human tendency is to focus on what's wrong and to forget what God has done for us. When ninety-nine out of a hundred things are going great in our lives, human nature will still focus on the *one* wrong thing. Our flesh tends to think that everything is falling apart even when all the evidence says we are blessed. Carnal human nature will always focus on the negative. This is something I fight against and hate to see in myself, so I tend to be a little too hard on others when they come to me with small problems that they have blown out of proportion.

One Monday morning, a long time ago, a student came into my office, crying. He was somebody who always focused on his problems. He was crying so hard, it took me five minutes to calm him down enough so he could start telling me what the problem was. It turned out to be a silly issue. He was upset because when he was in church the day before, two women seated in front of him had talked and laughed throughout the entire service. He felt like the devil used those women to steal the Word from him. So, I asked him, "Why didn't you move?" He'd never thought of that. He just sat through the entire service fuming with anger while binding and rebuking the devil.

Right before that student came into my office, I had just gotten off the phone with a friend of mine whose wife of fifty years died. I called him that morning to see how he was doing. He was praising God and thanking Him that he had been so happily married for fifty years! My friend was rejoicing and praising God in a circumstance that would have been a valid reason for sadness, while the student in my office was in tears because two people in front of him whispered during a church service.

I hate the natural tendency to get focused on the one little thing that is wrong in life. I don't like to see it in myself or in others. It will distort our perspective and keep us from seeing how blessed we truly are. When little problems come along, we have an inclination to magnify them until they take over our entire lives. We can reverse this tendency by thanking God and focusing on the good.

A friend of mine, Pastor Bob, has a daughter who hit her head in a car accident a number of years ago. Not long after the accident, she started getting a few headaches, and a couple of years later, she had a seizure. She was rushed to the hospital, but the doctors said she was brain-dead. They didn't expect her to live through the day. She was on all sorts of life-support equipment, and it didn't look good.

Soon, the doctor told Pastor Bob that his daughter was dead and that it was time to take her off the life-support equipment. He didn't get angry at what they said—he just told them he was going to keep believing God. She has been under twenty-four-hour care in their home for more than a decade now. The doctors still say she's brain-dead, but she's making progress.

Dealing with the long-term illness of a loved one tends to wear on people. At one of our *Ministers' Conferences*, Pastor Bob was sitting up front. I was preaching on how we magnify the negative and aren't appreciative for what we have and how we need to focus on the positive and glorify God. While I was talking, Pastor Bob stood up, threw his Bible on the floor, and said, "I've had all of this I can take. I just have to thank God for how good things are." He started praising, shouting, and glorifying the Lord. When the people in the room who knew his situation saw how thankful he was, they started hitting their knees and asking God to forgive them for being focused on insignificant problems. Pastor Bob is one of the happiest guys I know. He is always looking to see if there is anything he can do for you. He lives his life for other people—you will never hear him complain.

In March 2000, Pastor Bob's church—an $18-million facility—was destroyed in forty-five seconds when two tornadoes collided over it. A hundred people were in the building at the time, and every single one of them was supernaturally protected. Within thirty minutes, CNN was broadcasting an interview with Pastor Bob. He was standing in front of the destroyed facility, wearing a hard hat, and said, "God didn't do this. The devil did this. But we're going to come out of this better than before."

On the following Sunday, the local newspapers went to the auditorium that his church was holding services in temporarily, expecting to continue their report on the devastation caused by the church's collapse. One reporter told them he was expecting to hear people cry and talk about what was lost, but instead, the church members were acting as if they had won the lottery. People were running, jumping, and praising God because nobody was hurt during the tornadoes. They were also declaring how they were going to come out much better off than they were before this happened. Today they have a facility twice as nice, plus a brand-new building for their school with two gymnasiums—and everything is paid for!

Whatever we focus on is what we magnify. We have to stop magnifying the negative. As Christians, we should magnify God with thanksgiving; we should be a thankful people.

I don't believe we can use circumstances to discern what the will of God is. But if we look at scriptural examples, we will notice that when things are tough, it's a better indication that we're in the will of God. Just because we follow God doesn't mean that life is going to be all smooth sailing. Yet most people think that everything in life should be easy when they are serving God. I hate to break it to you, but that isn't what the Lord promised us. Jesus said, *"In the world ye shall have tribulation: but be of good cheer; I have overcome the world"* (John 16:33b).

God sent Paul and Silas into Macedonia, in the area of Philippi, and within days, they were beaten and in stocks (Acts 16:9-12 and 16-24). But they didn't cry and whine about the situation they were in. At midnight, they prayed and sang praises to God from their dungeon so all the prisoners could hear them. Suddenly, an earthquake shook the foundations of the prison, opened the doors, and broke open the prisoners' chains—that's a pretty unusual earthquake (Acts 16:25-26).

Praise is powerful! The amazing thing is that Paul and Silas didn't even try to go anywhere after the earthquake freed them. They weren't praising God just to get free or to get something from Him; they were praising God because they loved Him. They were actually excited about God even while they were in a rat-infested dungeon, their backs were bleeding, and they were facing possible execution.

A book entitled *Encyclopedia of Christian Martyrs* lists thousands of people who have been killed for their faith in Jesus. It tells about Christians during the Roman era who were so in love with the Lord that they would fight with each other to see who would get to go out and die for Jesus! Today most people can't wrap their brains around such desire.

One story tells of a woman who was eight months pregnant and awaiting execution in prison. All of her family and friends were going to be executed the next day in the Colosseum by having wild beasts turned on them. However, the Romans wouldn't kill a pregnant woman, so her execution would have to wait until after she gave birth. She knew they would kill her as soon as her baby was born. She wanted to die in unity with her friends, so she had her Christian brothers and sisters agree with her in prayer that the baby would be born early. She went into labor immediately and gave birth. A friend came to the prison to take her baby away, and she went out the next day to be executed with her friends. They stripped off her clothing, put her in a net, and turned wild bulls loose that ripped her to pieces. The entire time she was glorifying God and thanking Jesus for the honor of dying in His name.

Not many people today focus on the goodness of God to that degree. We sing about what a great day it will be when we all get to heaven, but when the doctor tells us we are dying, we start to cry. Dying and going to be with Jesus isn't something most Christians are excited about today, because most of us are more focused on the world than the things of God.

OUTLINE • 14.1

I. Believers should be getting stronger and stronger in the Lord as time goes on.

Because that, when they knew God, they glorified him not as God, neither were thankful; but became vain in their imaginations, and their foolish heart was darkened.

ROMANS 1:21

A. God never intended for the potency of our relationship with Him to fade, yet that is exactly what happens to many Christians.

B. The first step in staying sensitive to God and maintaining the intensity of our relationship with Him is to glorify Him—to value His opinion above the opinions of man.

C. In terms of practical living, however, glorifying God, being thankful, and having a godly imagination aren't separate issues; they are all interconnected.

D. So, this second step of thankfulness is something we add to our lifestyle of glorifying God in all circumstances.

I will praise the name of God with a song, and will magnify him with thanksgiving.

PSALM 69:30

E. Being thankful and rehearsing our victories makes God bigger in our perspective—it puts more glory, worth, and value on Him.

F. We should rehearse our victories on a regular basis.

   i.   In fact, this is the reason there are a number of scriptures in the Old Testament that commanded the Israelites not to take away their neighbor's landmark (Deut. 19:14, 27:17; Prov. 22:28, and 23:10).

   ii. Landmarks served as a reminder.

   iii. In the same way, we need to erect landmarks in our lives to remind us of the victories God has won for us.

Bless the LORD, O my soul: and all that is within me, bless his holy name. [2] Bless the LORD, O my soul, and forget not all his benefits.

PSALM 103:1-2

G. The reason this scripture tells us not to forget is because the natural human tendency is to focus on what's wrong and to forget what God has done for us.

H. When little problems come along, we have an inclination to magnify them until they take over our entire lives.

I. We can reverse this tendency by thanking God and focusing on the good (John 16:33).

TEACHER'S GUIDE • 14.1

1. Believers should be getting stronger and stronger in the Lord as time goes on. God never intended for the potency of our relationship with Him to fade, yet that is exactly what happens to many Christians. The first step in staying sensitive to God and maintaining the intensity of our relationship with Him is to glorify Him—to value His opinion above the opinions of man. In terms of practical living, however, glorifying God, being thankful, and having a godly imagination

> *Because that, when they knew God, they glorified him not as God, neither were thankful; but became vain in their imaginations, and their foolish heart was darkened.*
>
> ROMANS 1:21

aren't separate issues; they are all interconnected. So this second step of thankfulness is something we add to our lifestyle of glorifying God in all circumstances. Being thankful and rehearsing our victories makes God bigger in our perspective

> *I will praise the name of God with a song, and will magnify him with thanksgiving.*
>
> PSALM 69:30

—it puts more glory, worth, and value on Him. We should rehearse our victories on a regular basis. In fact, this is the reason there are a number of scriptures in the Old Testament that commanded the Israelites not to take away their neighbor's landmark (Deut. 19:14, 27:17; Prov. 22:28, and 23:10). Landmarks served as a reminder. In the same way, we need to erect landmarks in our lives to remind us of the victories God has won for us. The reason this scripture tells us not to forget

> *Bless the LORD, O my soul: and all that is within me, bless his holy name. [2] Bless the LORD, O my soul, and forget not all his benefits.*
>
> PSALM 103:1-2

is because the natural human tendency is to focus on what's wrong and to forget what God has done for us. When little problems come along, we have an inclination to magnify them until they take over our entire lives. We can reverse this tendency by thanking God and focusing on the good (John 16:33).

1a. True or false: Believers should be getting weaker and weaker in the Lord as time goes on.
False

1b. Romans 1:21 says, *"Because that, when they knew God, they glorified him not as God, neither were _____; but became _____ in their imaginations, and their _____ heart was darkened."*
"Thankful" / "vain" / "foolish"

1c. Discussion question: What are some practical ways that you can maintain the potency of your relationship with God?
Discussion question

1d.   *"I will praise the name of God with a song, and will _____"* (Ps. 69:30).
   A.   *"Play instruments to his glory"*
   B.   *"Magnify him with shouting"*
   C.   *"Magnify him with thanksgiving"*
   D.   All of the above
   E.   None of the above
   C.   *"Magnify him with thanksgiving"*

1e.   Discussion question: Meditate on Psalm 103:1-2 and share any thoughts and revelation you receive.
   Discussion question

1f.   Why does Psalm 103:2 tell you not to forget?
   Because the natural human tendency is to focus on what's wrong and to forget what God has done for you

DISCIPLESHIP QUESTIONS • 14.1

1. True or false: Believers should be getting weaker and weaker in the Lord as time goes on.

2. Romans 1:21 says, *"Because that, when they knew God, they glorified him not as God, neither were _____; but became _____ in their imaginations, and their _____ heart was darkened."*

3. Discussion question: What are some practical ways that you can maintain the potency of your relationship with God?

    _____

    _____

    _____

4. *"I will praise the name of God with a song, and will _____"* (Ps. 69:30).
    A. *"Play instruments to his glory"*
    B. *"Magnify him with shouting"*
    C. *"Magnify him with thanksgiving"*
    D. All of the above
    E. None of the above

5. Discussion question: Meditate on Psalm 103:1-2 and share any thoughts and revelation you receive.

    _____

    _____

    _____

6. Why does Psalm 103:2 tell you not to forget?

    _____

    _____

    _____

ANSWER KEY • 14.1

1. False
2. *"Thankful" / "vain" / "foolish"*
3. *Discussion question*
4. C. *"Magnify him with thanksgiving"*
5. *Discussion question*
6. Because the natural human tendency is to focus on what's wrong and to forget what God has done for you

ROMANS 1:21
Because that, when they knew God, they glorified him not as God, neither were thankful; but became vain in their imaginations, and their foolish heart was darkened.

PSALM 69:30
I will praise the name of God with a song, and will magnify him with thanksgiving.

DEUTERONOMY 19:14
Thou shalt not remove thy neighbour's landmark, which they of old time have set in thine inheritance, which thou shalt inherit in the land that the LORD thy God giveth thee to possess it.

DEUTERONOMY 27:17
Cursed be he that removeth his neighbour's landmark. And all the people shall say, Amen.

PROVERBS 22:28
Remove not the ancient landmark, which thy fathers have set.

PROVERBS 23:10
Remove not the old landmark; and enter not into the fields of the fatherless.

1 SAMUEL 7:12
Then Samuel took a stone, and set it between Mizpeh and Shen, and called the name of it Ebenezer, saying, Hitherto hath the LORD helped us.

PSALM 116:6
The LORD preserveth the simple: I was brought low, and he helped me.

LUKE 19:40
And he answered and said unto them, I tell you that, if these should hold their peace, the stones would immediately cry out.

PSALM 103:1-2
Bless the LORD, O my soul: and all that is within me, bless his holy name. [2] Bless the LORD, O my soul, and forget not all his benefits.

JOHN 16:33
These things I have spoken unto you, that in me ye might have peace. In the world ye shall have tribulation: but be of good cheer; I have overcome the world.

ACTS 16:9-12

And a vision appeared to Paul in the night; There stood a man of Macedonia, and prayed him, saying, Come over into Macedonia, and help us. [10] And after he had seen the vision, immediately we endeavoured to go into Macedonia, assuredly gathering that the Lord had called us for to preach the gospel unto them. [11] Therefore loosing from Troas, we came with a straight course to Samothracia, and the next day to Neapolis; [12] And from thence to Philippi, which is the chief city of that part of Macedonia, and a colony: and we were in that city abiding certain days.

ACTS 16:16-26

And it came to pass, as we went to prayer, a certain damsel possessed with a spirit of divination met us, which brought her masters much gain by soothsaying: [17] The same followed Paul and us, and cried, saying, These men are the servants of the most high God, which shew unto us the way of salvation. [18] And this did she many days. But Paul, being grieved, turned and said to the spirit, I command thee in the name of Jesus Christ to come out of her. And he came out the same hour. [19] And when her masters saw that the hope of their gains was gone, they caught Paul and Silas, and drew them into the marketplace unto the rulers, [20] And brought them to the magistrates, saying, These men, being Jews, do exceedingly trouble our city, [21] And teach customs, which are not lawful for us to receive, neither to observe, being Romans. [22] And the multitude rose up together against them: and the magistrates rent off their clothes, and commanded to beat them. [23] And when they had laid many stripes upon them, they cast them into prison, charging the jailor to keep them safely: [24] Who, having received such a charge, thrust them into the inner prison, and made their feet fast in the stocks. [25] And at midnight Paul and Silas prayed, and sang praises unto God: and the prisoners heard them. [26] And suddenly there was a great earthquake, so that the foundations of the prison were shaken: and immediately all the doors were opened, and every one's bands were loosed.

LESSON 14.2

This know also, that in the last days perilous times shall come. [2] For men shall be lovers of their own selves, covetous, boasters, proud, blasphemers, disobedient to parents, unthankful, unholy, [3] Without natural affection, trucebreakers, false accusers, incontinent, fierce, despisers of those that are good, [4] Traitors, heady, highminded, lovers of pleasures more than lovers of God.

2 TIMOTHY 3:1-4

I don't know if you have figured this out or not, but we are living in the last days. The Apostle Peter said that the last days began over 2,000 years ago on the Day of Pentecost (Acts 2:17), which puts us in the *last* of the last days. Scripture says that in the last days, people will become lovers of themselves—and most people today are very self-centered. The very reason our lives are miserable is because we love ourselves so much. Self-love is like an addiction; you can't get enough of it. The more you get, the more you want. You can't satisfy self; self has to be denied. You need to get beyond thinking only of yourself. When you are all wrapped up in yourself, you make a very small package.

In the end times, it says people will be covetous. Westerners are probably the most covetous people on the face of the earth. We have been taught to grab all we can—like a vacuum cleaner sucking up everything in its path. The American dream is to accumulate more and more. I'm not trying to make anyone feel condemned; I'm just pointing out the reality of where our society is today. Western society is very covetous. The Bible teaches us that covetousness is idolatry (Col. 3:5). Most covetous people wouldn't say they are idol worshipers—but they are, and it's a sign of the end times.

In the last days, people will be boasters. I've seen this change come about in my own lifetime. At the core, people are the same as they have always been, but they haven't always been so bold in their boasting. Back when I was young, people didn't go around announcing how awesome they were. It would have been considered pride—that kind of behavior was frowned upon. Nowadays, society seems to admire pride and boasting. People generally think it's a good thing to act like they're awesome and that the world revolves around them. Sadly, even a lot of Christians act like that; they are boasters. They're proud. These negative traits are very descriptive of our world today.

Next, the Scripture says people will become blasphemers. I've noticed that even the conservative talk show hosts on the radio, who are supposed to be counterculture to the liberal media, use profanity on a regular basis. Words that would have been considered completely unacceptable in conversation when I was a kid are used all the time—and people don't think anything about it.

The Scripture says children will be disobedient to parents. Is there anyone who doubts that children today are probably more disobedient to parents and more rebellious than ever?

The verse also says that in the last days, people will be unthankful and unholy. Look at the list that being unthankful is put in. It's sandwiched right in there with people who lack natural affection and who are trucebreakers, false accusers, incontinent, fierce, despisers of those who are good, traitors, heady, high-minded, and lovers of pleasures more than lovers of God. Families are falling apart today because people don't have the natural love that should bind a family together; they are too selfish. The word *"incontinent"* in this verse means having totally unrestrained emotions. People today are totally dominated and controlled by their emotions. Finally, the Scripture says that people will be lovers of pleasure more than lovers of God. Without a doubt, people spend way more time and money on pleasure than they do on God.

Being unthankful is listed right in the midst of all these terrible traits that describe the end times we are living in. We are too focused on the negative. If we want to finish our course and fulfill our destiny, one of the things we can do to keep our hearts in the right place is to make the decision to bless the Lord at all times. We can get to a place where we are so positive that no matter what happens to us, we will find something to praise God about— not that we won't have problems, but in the light of eternity, our problems are no big deal.

Eternal Perspective

For our light affliction, which is but for a moment, worketh for us a far more exceeding and eternal weight of glory; [18] While we look not at the things which are seen, but at the things which are not seen: for the things which are seen are temporal; but the things which are not seen are eternal.
2 CORINTHIANS 4:17-18

Paul called his trials a *"light affliction,"* yet he had a lot more problems than we do (2 Cor. 11:23-27). He was beaten with rods three times—the punishment of lifting a prisoner off the ground and beating the back of his calves, feet, and ankles with rods until the bones were broken. He said he was whipped so many times, he couldn't count them all. He was imprisoned and persecuted more than any other person in Scripture. When I go to a city to preach the Gospel, I usually stay in a nice hotel. Paul, on the other hand, would end up in stocks in the lowest part of the dungeon. He endured tremendous persecution and rejection.

If Paul could call his persecution a *"light affliction,"* how can we believe our problems are such a heavy burden? It's because we don't have the same perspective that Paul had. As I said, our minds are like a pair of binoculars: Whatever we focus on gets bigger. We can either magnify the little negative things, or by turning the binoculars around, we can look through the big end, and even a huge mountain will shrink down to nothing. What we focus our attention on becomes bigger, and what we neglect becomes smaller.

Paul was so focused on God that he could say, *"For to me to live is Christ, and to die is gain"* (Phil. 1:21). One of the ways you can get the same perspective is to remember that your afflictions are *"but for a moment."* Take any problem you might have right now, and put it into the perspective of eternity. A thousand years from now, will whatever is bothering you still be a problem? No, not even if your problems are life threatening! Everyone is going to die. You might live forty, sixty, or eighty years, but everyone is going to die, unless Jesus comes back during this lifetime. You shouldn't be hanging on to this life like it's all you have. When you die, you go to be with the Lord. It's going to be awesome! The sufferings of this world are not even worthy to be compared with the glory that will be revealed when you go to be with Jesus (Rom. 8:18).

I take care of my body by exercising and eating right because I believe I have a mission to complete, but if I was to die tomorrow, it wouldn't bother me one bit. I'm making a difference through my life and ministry, but I'm also excited about going to be with the Lord. It wouldn't bother me at all to check out, amen. God would get somebody else to carry on what I'm doing. He would work it all out. Once you get that attitude, once you put things into an eternal perspective, the troubles you have in this life will shrink down to nothing in comparison.

I remember a woman who approached me for prayer one day after I finished preaching. She was crying as she told me that she was on her fourth marriage—and her current husband wanted to divorce her. She couldn't stand the idea of getting divorced again, so she'd tried to commit suicide the day before.

She said, "I'm not a Christian like you, but I know God is real and that prayer works. Would you please pray for me that I won't get divorced?"

"You're not a Christian," I asked, "and you know that you aren't a Christian?"

"Yes," she answered.

"And you want me to pray for your marriage, but you don't want to be born again?"

"That's right," she said.

I just looked at her for a moment. "Don't you realize that after you've burned in hell for a thousand years, you won't give a rip whether your marriage worked or not?" I said, "Who cares about your marriage?"

She looked like I had just slapped her in the face. She quit crying, looked at me, and said, "You know, I think you're right. I need to get saved."

"You sure do," I said. We prayed, she was born again, and *then* we prayed for her marriage.

I'm not saying God doesn't care about marriages; I'm saying that some people think that whatever hardship they are going through exempts them from the need to rejoice. It doesn't. Our salvation is more important than our marriages, health, or anything else. We aren't supposed to be happy about tragedy, but tragedy doesn't undo the goodness of God. Even when somebody dies, if they were a Christian, we can rejoice that they're in the presence of the Lord. It's normal to miss a person when they die, but the grief we feel is for us. There is no reason to feel sorry for somebody who has died and gone to be with the Lord. It doesn't matter if they died in an accident or prematurely; they are in the presence of God. It helps to understand that the grief we feel is for our own sense of loss. We need to recognize that the person is in heaven. It shrinks the loss down when it's put into the light of eternity.

Having an eternal perspective will change your way of thinking about everything. If the doctor tells you that you are going to die, it won't be a big deal. The Bible says that God wants people well (3 John 2) and it's His will to heal everyone (Acts 10:38), but the worst-case scenario is that you go to be with the Lord (2 Cor. 5:8). Having an eternal perspective rids you of fear, stress, and worry. The Bible also says that a merry heart does good like a medicine (Prov. 17:22). You could thank God that you're in a win-win situation: When you get healed, you can travel the world telling people how God healed you; but if for some reason you don't get healed, then you get to go be with the Lord. You can't lose for winning.

As you start being thankful and magnifying God, your immune system will work better, and you will probably see your healing manifest. You win by becoming a thankful person. Start by thanking God every morning just for being alive.

Everything you can see is temporary: your house, car, clothes—everything. But the things you can't see are eternal. Paul wasn't just looking at the natural realm. He wasn't focused on his house, assets, or retirement; he was looking at intangible, eternal things—that's how you fulfill God's will for your life.

Jesus is the same yesterday, today, and forever (Heb. 13:8). If your focus and value are on the Lord, you won't fluctuate with circumstances. Joy that comes and goes is a sign that you aren't focused on God. You don't have to live like an unbeliever, just trying to satisfy your carnal desires. You can live to glorify God. You can thank God every day. Maybe events in your life aren't perfect, but you can always find something to praise God for.

Being thankful is how we fight against the natural human tendency to focus on problems. Actually, being thankful and glorifying God are very closely related. We can't truly glorify God unless we are thankful. Our carnal nature tends toward forgetting the goodness of God. One of the things we must do to stay thankful is rehearse our victories and remember the good things God has done for us. *Problems are going to come, but having an eternal perspective will give us the momentum to roll right over trouble.*

If we are traveling at a thousand miles per hour, the devil can put a brick wall in our path, and it won't stop us. In the same way, we can build up so much momentum in our Christian lives that no problem can take away our joy or keep us from glorifying God. To fulfill God's will, we are going to have to develop this attitude. We need to glorify God and keep our hearts sensitive to Him by being thankful—then we will see that life works much better.

OUTLINE • 14.2

II. The Apostle Peter said that the last days began over 2,000 years ago on the Day of Pentecost (Acts 2:17), which puts us in the *last* of the last days.

This know also, that in the last days perilous times shall come. [2] For men shall be lovers of their own selves, covetous, boasters, proud, blasphemers, disobedient to parents, unthankful, unholy, [3] Without natural affection, trucebreakers, false accusers, incontinent, fierce, despisers of those that are good, [4] Traitors, heady, highminded, lovers of pleasures more than lovers of God.

2 TIMOTHY 3:1-4

A. Scripture says that in the last days, people will become lovers of themselves—and most people today are very self-centered.

    i. Self-love is like an addiction; no one can get enough of it.

    ii. We can't satisfy self; self has to be denied.

B. In the end times, it says people will be covetous.

    i. The Bible teaches us that covetousness is idolatry (Col. 3:5).

    ii. Most covetous people wouldn't say they are idol worshipers—but they are.

C. In the last days, people will be boasters.

    i. People generally think it's a good thing to act like they're awesome and the world revolves around them.

    ii. Sadly, even a lot of Christians act like that; they are boasters.

D. Next, the Scripture says people will become blasphemers, children will be disobedient to parents, and people will be unthankful and unholy.

    i. Let's look at the list that being unthankful is put in: It's sandwiched right in there with people who lack natural affection and who are trucebreakers, false accusers, incontinent, fierce, despisers of those who are good, traitors, heady, high-minded, and lovers of pleasures more than lovers of God.

        a. The word *"incontinent"* in this verse means having totally unrestrained emotions.

        b. People today are totally dominated and controlled by their emotions.

E. Finally, the Scripture says that people will be lovers of pleasure more than lovers of God.

    i. Without a doubt, people spend way more time and money on pleasure than they do on God.

F.   If we want to finish our course and fulfill our destiny, one of the things we can do to keep our hearts in the right place is to make the decision to bless the Lord at all times.

G.   We can get to a place where we are so positive that no matter what happens to us, we will find something to praise God about.

III.   Paul called his trials a *"light affliction,"* yet he had a lot more problems than we do (2 Cor. 11:23-27)—he endured tremendous persecution and rejection.

For our light affliction, which is but for a moment, worketh for us a far more exceeding and eternal weight of glory; [18] While we look not at the things which are seen, but at the things which are not seen: for the things which are seen are temporal; but the things which are not seen are eternal.

2 CORINTHIANS 4:17-18

A.   If Paul could call his persecution a *"light affliction,"* how can we believe our problems are such a heavy burden?

B.   It's because we don't have the same perspective that Paul had.

C.   Paul was so focused on God that he could say, *"For to me to live is Christ, and to die is gain"* (Phil. 1:21).

D.   One of the ways we can get the same perspective is to remember that our afflictions are *"but for a moment."*

E.   We can take any problem we might have right now and put it into the perspective of eternity.

F.   The sufferings of this world are not even worthy to be compared with the glory that will be revealed when we go to be with Jesus (Rom. 8:18).

G.   Having an eternal perspective will change our way of thinking about everything.

H.   Maybe events in our lives aren't perfect, but we can always find something to praise God for.

I.   Being thankful is how we fight against the natural human tendency to focus on problems.

J.   *Problems are going to come, but having an eternal perspective will give us the momentum to roll right over trouble.*

K.   We can build up so much momentum in our Christian lives that no problem can take away our joy or keep us from glorifying God.

2. The Apostle Peter said that the last days began over 2,000 years ago on the Day of Pentecost (Acts 2:17), which puts us in the *last* of the last days.

> *This know also, that in the last days perilous times shall come. [2] For men shall be lovers of their own selves, covetous, boasters, proud, blasphemers, disobedient to parents, unthankful, unholy, [3] Without natural affection, trucebreakers, false accusers, incontinent, fierce, despisers of those that are good, [4] Traitors, heady, highminded, lovers of pleasures more than lovers of God.*
>
> 2 TIMOTHY 3:1-4

Scripture says that in the last days, people will become lovers of themselves—and most people today are very self-centered. Self-love is like an addiction; no one can get enough of it. We can't satisfy self; self has to be denied. In the end times, it says people will be covetous. The Bible teaches us that covetousness is idolatry (Col. 3:5). Most covetous people wouldn't say they are idol worshipers—but they are. In the last days, people will be boasters. People generally think it's a good thing to act like they're awesome and the world revolves around them. Sadly, even a lot of Christians act like that; they are boasters. Next, the Scripture says people will become blasphemers, children will be disobedient to parents, and people will be unthankful and unholy. Let's look at the list that being unthankful is put in: It's sandwiched right in there with people who lack natural affection and who are trucebreakers, false accusers, incontinent, fierce, despisers of those who are good, traitors, heady, high-minded, and lovers of pleasures more than lovers of God. The word *"incontinent"* in this verse means having totally unrestrained emotions. People today are totally dominated and controlled by their emotions. Finally, the Scripture says that people will be lovers of pleasure more than lovers of God. Without a doubt, people spend way more time and money on pleasure than they do on God. If we want to finish our course and fulfill our destiny, one of the things we can do to keep our hearts in the right place is to make the decision to bless the Lord at all times. We can get to a place where we are so positive that no matter what happens to us, we will find something to praise God about.

2a. List at least four of the traits of people that 2 Timothy 3:2-4 says are characteristics of the last days.
"Lovers of their own selves, covetous, boasters, proud, blasphemers, disobedient to parents, unthankful, unholy, without natural affection, trucebreakers, false accusers, incontinent, fierce, despisers of those that are good, traitors, heady, highminded, lovers of pleasures more than lovers of God"

2b. Discussion question: Have you seen any evidence in your life that self does have to be denied? How have you handled those situations?
Discussion question

2c. Which scripture says that covetousness is idolatry?
Colossians 3:5

2d. Discussion question: What do you think that scripture means by that (i.e., covetousness is idolatry)?
Discussion question

2e. Discussion question: Why do you think being unthankful was put into the same list as false accusers, traitors, despisers of those who are good, high-minded, etc.?
Discussion question

2f. People spend way more _____ and _____ on pleasure than they do on God.
Time / money

2g. You can get to a place where you are so positive that no matter what happens to you, what will happen?
You will find something to praise God about

3. Paul called his trials a *"light affliction,"* yet he had a lot more problems than we do (2 Cor. 11:23-27)—he endured tremendous persecution and rejection.

> *For our light affliction, which is but for a moment, worketh for us a far more exceeding and eternal weight of glory;* **[18]** *While we look not at the things which are seen, but at the things which are not seen: for the things which are seen are temporal; but the things which are not seen are eternal.*
>
> 2 CORINTHIANS 4:17-18

If Paul could call his persecution a *"light affliction,"* how can we believe our problems are such a heavy burden? It's because we don't have the same perspective that Paul had. Paul was so focused on God that he could say, *"For to me to live is Christ, and to die is gain"* (Phil. 1:21). One of the ways we can get the same perspective is to remember that our afflictions are *"but for a moment."* We can take any problem we might have right now and put it into the perspective of eternity. The sufferings of this world are not even worthy to be compared with the glory that will be revealed when we go to be with Jesus (Rom. 8:18). Having an eternal perspective will change our way of thinking about everything. Maybe events in our lives aren't perfect, but we can always find something to praise God for. Being thankful is how we fight against the natural human tendency to focus on problems. *Problems are going to come, but having an eternal perspective will give us the momentum to roll right over trouble.* We can build up so much momentum in our Christian lives that no problem can take away our joy or keep us from glorifying God.

3a.   How did Paul refer to his trials?
    A.   As nothing to worry about
    B.   As a hard burden to bear
    C.   As suffering for Jesus
    D.   All of the above
    E.   None of the above
    E.   None of the above

3b.   What is one of the ways you can get the same perspective Paul had?
    To remember that your afflictions are *"but for a moment"*

3c.   Discussion question: Take one of the problems you are facing now, and put it in the light of eternity. How does that change your attitude in the matter?
    Discussion question

3d.   What does Romans 8:18 tell you?
    That the sufferings of this world are not even worthy to be compared with the glory that will be revealed when you go to be with Jesus

3e.   Discussion question: What are some things in your life for which you can praise God?
    Discussion question

3f.   _____ is how you fight against the natural tendency to focus on problems.
    Being thankful

7. List at least four of the traits of people that 2 Timothy 3:2-4 says are characteristics of the last days.

_____

_____

_____

8. Discussion question: Have you seen any evidence in your life that self does have to be denied? How have you handled those situations?

_____

_____

_____

9. Which scripture says that covetousness is idolatry?

_____

_____

_____

10. Discussion question: What do you think that scripture means by that (i.e., covetousness is idolatry)?

_____

_____

_____

11. Discussion question: Why do you think being unthankful was put into the same list as false accusers, traitors, despisers of those who are good, high-minded, etc.?

_____

_____

_____

12. People spend way more _____ and _____ on pleasure than they do on God.

13. You can get to a place where you are so positive that no matter what happens to you, what will happen?

_____

_____

_____

14. How did Paul refer to his trials?
    A. As nothing to worry about
    B. As a hard burden to bear
    C. As suffering for Jesus
    D. All of the above
    E. None of the above

15. What is one of the ways you can get the same perspective Paul had?

_____

_____

_____

16. Discussion question: Take one of the problems you are facing now, and put it in the light of eternity. How does that change your attitude in the matter?

_____

_____

_____

17. What does Romans 8:18 tell you?

_____

_____

_____

18. Discussion question: What are some things in your life for which you can praise God?

_____

_____

_____

19. _____ is how you fight against the natural tendency to focus on problems.

7. *"Lovers of their own selves, covetous, boasters, proud, blasphemers, disobedient to parents, unthankful, unholy, without natural affection, trucebreakers, false accusers, incontinent, fierce, despisers of those that are good, traitors, heady, highminded, lovers of pleasures more than lovers of God"*

8. *Discussion question*

9. Colossians 3:5

10. *Discussion question*

11. *Discussion question*

12. Time / money

13. You will find something to praise God about

14. E. None of the above

15. To remember that your afflictions are *"but for a moment"*

16. *Discussion question*

17. That the sufferings of this world are not even worthy to be compared with the glory that will be revealed when you go to be with Jesus

18. *Discussion question*

19. Being thankful

2 TIMOTHY 3:1-4

This know also, that in the last days perilous times shall come. [2] For men shall be lovers of their own selves, covetous, boasters, proud, blasphemers, disobedient to parents, unthankful, unholy, [3] Without natural affection, trucebreakers, false accusers, incontinent, fierce, despisers of those that are good, [4] Traitors, heady, highminded, lovers of pleasures more than lovers of God.

ACTS 2:17

And it shall come to pass in the last days, saith God, I will pour out of my Spirit upon all flesh: and your sons and your daughters shall prophesy, and your young men shall see visions, and your old men shall dream dreams.

COLOSSIANS 3:5

Mortify therefore your members which are upon the earth; fornication, uncleanness, inordinate affection, evil concupiscence, and covetousness, which is idolatry.

2 CORINTHIANS 4:17-18

For our light affliction, which is but for a moment, worketh for us a far more exceeding and eternal weight of glory; [18] While we look not at the things which are seen, but at the things which are not seen: for the things which are seen are temporal; but the things which are not seen are eternal.

2 CORINTHIANS 11:23-27

Are they ministers of Christ? (I speak as a fool) I am more; in labours more abundant, in stripes above measure, in prisons more frequent, in deaths oft. [24] Of the Jews five times received I forty stripes save one. [25] Thrice was I beaten with rods, once was I stoned, thrice I suffered shipwreck, a night and a day I have been in the deep; [26] In journeyings often, in perils of waters, in perils of robbers, in perils by mine own countrymen, in perils by the heathen, in perils in the city, in perils in the wilderness, in perils in the sea, in perils among false brethren; [27] In weariness and painfulness, in watchings often, in hunger and thirst, in fastings often, in cold and nakedness.

PHILIPPIANS 1:21

For to me to live is Christ, and to die is gain.

ROMANS 8:18

For I reckon that the sufferings of this present time are not worthy to be compared with the glory which shall be revealed in us.

3 JOHN 2
Beloved, I wish above all things that thou mayest prosper and be in health, even as thy soul prospereth.

ACTS 10:38
How God anointed Jesus of Nazareth with the Holy Ghost and with power: who went about doing good, and healing all that were oppressed of the devil; for God was with him.

2 CORINTHIANS 5:8
We are confident, I say, and willing rather to be absent from the body, and to be present with the Lord.

PROVERBS 17:22
A merry heart doeth good like a medicine: but a broken spirit drieth the bones.

HEBREWS 13:8
Jesus Christ the same yesterday, and to day, and for ever.

PUTTING YOUR IMAGINATION TO WORK

LESSON 15.1

Because that, when they knew God, they glorified him not as God, neither were thankful; but became vain in their imaginations, and their foolish heart was darkened.

ROMANS 1:21

This verse reveals that the last step in hardening your heart toward God is becoming vain in your imagination. Again, the steps we have been discussing are not disconnected. Knowing God but failing to glorify Him, being unthankful, and having a vain imagination are sequential steps in the process of walking away from the Lord. The first thing that happens is you let something other than God occupy your attention and start valuing the opinions of others above God. After you stop glorifying God, you become unthankful, and finally your imagination becomes vain. *This doesn't mean your imagination stops working—it means it starts working against you.* It might mean you start imagining failure instead of success. One thing leads to another, and the end result is a hardened heart.

Adults often wrongly believe that using their imagination is the same as fantasizing, but it isn't. *Imagination* is defined as "the act or power of forming a mental image of something not present to the senses or never before wholly perceived in reality" (*Merriam-Webster Dictionary*). For example, you probably haven't counted how many doors are in your house. But if I asked you how many doors were in your house, you could bring up a mental image of your house and count the doors by going through the picture in your mind (imagination). You aren't seeing the space with your physical eyes; you are using your imagination. You do the same thing when someone asks you for directions, and you visualize the route in your mind as you give instructions. *Imagination is the ability to see something with your mind, or your heart, that you can't see with your eyes.*

We can't function in our daily lives without using our imagination. We think in pictures. When the word "apple" is spoken, we don't envision the letters a-p-p-l-e; we see a mental image of an apple. Some people might see a green apple, while others see a red apple, but the word "apple" still brings an image to mind. We can't really understand something until we can picture it in our minds, which is why people say a picture is worth a thousand words. If we can picture something, we can do it!

In Vietnam we got our water from *water blivets*. Most of you can't picture a water blivet; therefore, you won't be able to remember this or describe it to others. Water blivets are black cylinder-looking rubber containers with brass ends. They were flown in to us by helicopters in 250-, 500-, 1,000-gallon sizes. Each had a spigot on the end we used to fill our water containers. As the water came out, the atmospheric pressure would collapse the blivet, and it would become flat. Then the helicopter would pick it up and carry it away.

You still may not have a great picture of a water blivet, but the words I used to describe it painted a picture in your imagination, so now you have some concept of what a water blivet is. You will be able to remember what it is because you have an image to attach it to.

This is why architects use blueprints: to show the builders how to construct what they have imagined. Our ministry is in the process of designing buildings for construction at our new campus in Woodland Park, Colorado. We sat together for hours talking about how we want the auditorium to look. It's a process of forming a mental image. Once we were able to picture in our imagination what we wanted, the architects could put it together.

Imagination is further defined as "creative ability" and "resourcefulness" (*Merriam-Webster Dictionary*). You can't create without an imagination. Not long ago, I built a deck at my house. I'm not an experienced builder; I just wanted the challenge of building something, so I constructed a three-level deck. While I was planning, I used to sit on a bucket and imagine what I wanted the deck to look like. I didn't have a blueprint or anything. I just pictured it in my mind. After I was able to imagine it on the inside, I was able to build it.

Imagination isn't just for little kids. You can't function without it. Imagination helps you understand abstract concepts like mathematics. Some people struggle with comprehending math, but a good teacher will illustrate math problems in a way that helps students understand. Instead of saying "two plus two equals four," they will draw a word picture, like "If you have two pieces of apple pie on your plate and you add two pieces of peach pie, how many pieces of pie are on your plate?" People will begin to see the relevance if you can get them to picture the concept in their minds. A good teacher is someone who paints pictures with words and helps the listener to visualize ideas.

You can't see anything happen without your imagination. If you can't see something on the inside, you won't be able to see it manifest in your life. If you can't see yourself healed or imagine yourself healthy, you won't see healing manifest in your body. A lot of people know that God can heal, but in their imagination, they see themselves as sick. They see themselves suffering and in pain. Some people have been sick for so long that they even see themselves being sick in their dreams. Their imagination is still working, but it's working against them; it has become vain.

Memory is also tied to imagination—from simple things like remembering where you parked your car to recalling the neighborhood you grew up in. Most people don't write down where they parked their car when they go somewhere. They don't remember specific instructions like: take a left turn after the lamp post, walk ten steps, and turn right, bear left, etc. They just have a mental image of where they left their car. In the same way, you have a mental image of where you grew up.

Sometimes, the image we have is different from reality. I grew up not too far from a patch of woods that I used to play in as a little kid. I remember riding my bike into the cool darkness during summer and having to wait while my eyes adjusted. It was a special place to me. As an adult, I recalled that space being miles and miles wide, but when I went back and saw it later in life, it was just one small acre of trees. The woods had grown in my memory over time, because images inside of us can be affected or polluted by a lot of different factors.

The word "imagination" and variations of "imagine" are used thirty-six times in the Bible. One of the words translated as "imagination" is the Hebrew word *yetser*. *Yetser* was also translated *"mind"* in the Scripture: *"Thou wilt keep him in perfect peace, whose mind is stayed on thee: because he trusteth in thee"* (Is. 26:3). When it says "keep your mind stayed on the Lord," it's talking about more than just having thoughts concerning God; it means to think about God until it paints an image on the inside of you, and you begin to see things from His perspective. This is why many people don't understand the power that's in the Word of God. They only look on the surface level. They may get a glimpse of something, but they don't meditate on it until they see it clearly on the inside.

Imagination is a very important concept to understand; it is one of the things that will allow us to fulfill God's will. Believers can't live having a surface-level understanding of the things of God. We have to go beyond the surface, to the point where the Word of God literally changes the way we see things with our hearts.

I heard a story about a pastor's wife who was almost blind. Her glasses were so thick that they looked like the bottom of a soda bottle. A healing evangelist was preaching at their church one day, so she was trying to avoid him. Many people had prayed for her eyes in the past, but her eyes had never been healed, and she didn't want to go through that whole experience again. But the healing evangelist cornered her at one of the services.

"I want to pray for you," he said.

He made her take her glasses off and commanded her eyes to be healed. When he was done, he asked, "Can you see?"

The woman started to open her eyes to check her vision, but the healing evangelist stopped her. "Shut your eyes!" he ordered.

She shut her eyes quickly.

"Can you see?" he asked.

As soon as she started to open her eyes, he commanded again, "Shut your eyes!"

They repeated the same exchange a third time. Confused, she was standing there with her eyes closed wondering, *What is this man doing? How can I tell if I can see if I don't open my eyes?*

Then she heard the evangelist say, "I didn't tell you to open your eyes. You have to see yourself seeing on the inside, before you can see it on the outside."

She stood there with her eyes closed, thinking about what he said. Within a few minutes, she understood what he was asking her. He was asking, *"Can you see yourself seeing? In your imagination, are you blind or can you see?"*

She prayed in tongues for a while and finally said, "I can see myself seeing."

"Now open your eyes," he told her.

When she opened her eyes, her vision was perfect.

OUTLINE • 15.1

I. Romans 1:21 reveals that the last step in hardening your heart toward God is becoming vain in your imagination.

> *Because that, when they knew God, they glorified him not as God, neither were thankful; but became vain in their imaginations, and their foolish heart was darkened.*
>
> ROMANS 1:21

A. *This doesn't mean your imagination stops working—it means it starts working against you.*

B. *Imagination* is defined as "the act or power of forming a mental image of something not present to the senses or never before wholly perceived in reality" (*Merriam-Webster Dictionary*).

C. *Imagination is the ability to see something with your mind, or your heart, that you can't see with your eyes.*

D. You can't function in your daily life without using your imagination—you think in pictures.

E. You can't really understand something until you can picture it in your mind.

F. If you can picture something, you can do it!

G. Imagination is further defined as "creative ability" and "resourcefulness" (*Merriam-Webster Dictionary*)—you can't create without an imagination.

H. If you can't see something on the inside, you won't be able to see it manifest in your life (like healing).

I. *Yetser*—the Hebrew word translated "imagination" in the Old Testament—was also translated "*mind*": "*Thou wilt keep him in perfect peace, whose mind is stayed on thee: because he trusteth in thee*" (Is. 26:3).

J. When it says "keep your mind stayed on the Lord," it's talking about more than just having thoughts concerning God; it means to think about God until it paints an image on the inside of you, and you begin to see things from His perspective.

K. Imagination is a very important concept to understand; it is one of the things that will allow you to fulfill God's will.

L. You have to go beyond the surface, to the point where the Word of God literally changes the way you see things with your heart.

TEACHER'S GUIDE • 15.1

1. Romans 1:21 reveals that the last step in hardening your heart toward God is becoming vain in your imagination.

> *Because that, when they knew God, they glorified him not as God, neither were thankful; but became vain in their imaginations, and their foolish heart was darkened.*
>
> ROMANS 1:21

This doesn't mean your imagination stops working—it means it starts working against you. Imagination is defined as "the act or power of forming a mental image of something not present to the senses or never before wholly perceived in reality" (*Merriam-Webster Dictionary*). *Imagination is the ability to see something with your mind, or your heart, that you can't see with your eyes.* You can't function in your daily life without using your imagination—you think in pictures. You can't really understand something until you can picture it in your mind. If you can picture something, you can do it! Imagination is further defined as "creative ability" and "resourcefulness" (*Merriam-Webster Dictionary*)—you can't create without an imagination. If you can't see something on the inside, you won't be able to see it manifest in your life (like healing). *Yetser*—the Hebrew word translated "imagination" in the Old Testament—was also translated *"mind": "Thou wilt keep him in perfect peace, whose mind is stayed on thee: because he trusteth in thee"* (Is. 26:3). When it says "keep your mind stayed on the Lord," it's talking about more than just having thoughts concerning God: It means to think about God until it paints an image on the inside of you and you begin to see things from His perspective. Imagination is a very important concept to understand; it is one of the things that will allow you to fulfill God's will. You have to go beyond the surface, to the point where the Word of God literally changes the way you see things with your heart.

1a. According to Romans 1:21, what is the last step in hardening your heart toward God?
   Becoming vain in your imagination

1b. What does it mean to have a vain imagination?
   Your imagination starts working against you

1c. Discussion question: Has your imagination ever been vain? In what ways?
   Discussion question

1d. What is imagination?
   "The act or power of forming a mental image of something not present to the senses or never before wholly perceived in reality" (*Merriam-Webster Dictionary*); the ability to see something with your mind, or heart, that you can't see with your eyes; "creative ability" and "resourcefulness" (*Merriam-Webster Dictionary*)

1e. True or false: If you can't see something on the inside, you will be able to see it manifest in your life.
   False

1f.   Discussion question: What does it mean to you to "keep your mind stayed on the Lord" (Is. 26:3)?
Discussion question

DISCIPLESHIP QUESTIONS • 15.1

1. According to Romans 1:21, what is the last step in hardening your heart toward God?

_____

_____

_____

2. What does it mean to have a vain imagination?

_____

_____

_____

3. Discussion question: Has your imagination ever been vain? In what ways?

_____

_____

_____

4. What is imagination?

_____

_____

_____

5. True or false: If you can't see something on the inside, you will be able to see it manifest in your life.

6. Discussion question: What does it mean to you to "keep your mind stayed on the Lord" (Is. 26:3)?

_____

_____

_____

ANSWER KEY • 15.1

1. Becoming vain in your imagination
2. It means that your imagination starts working against you
3. *Discussion question*
4. "The act or power of forming a mental image of something not present to the senses or never before wholly perceived in reality" (*Merriam-Webster Dictionary*); the ability to see something with your mind, or heart, that you can't see with your eyes; "creative ability" and "resourcefulness" (*Merriam-Webster Dictionary*)
5. False
6. *Discussion question*

ROMANS 1:21

Because that, when they knew God, they glorified him not as God, neither were thankful; but became vain in their imaginations, and their foolish heart was darkened.

ISAIAH 26:3

Thou wilt keep him in perfect peace, whose mind is stayed on thee: because he trusteth in thee.

LESSON 15.2

A lot of people miss what God has for them because even though they ask for healing, they see themselves as sick. They have been sick for so long that the sickness is not just in their bodies—the sickness has spread to their minds and emotions. When they pray, they are hoping something will happen, but they don't really believe it on the inside. They don't see themselves well on the inside. Their imaginations have become vain and are working against them: They see themselves as sick and don't really believe anything is going to change.

Now faith is the substance of things hoped for, the evidence of things not seen.
HEBREWS 11:1

Hope is your *imagination* (Rom. 8:24-25), and faith is the *substance* of things hoped for. If you can't hope for something first (i.e., imagine it), then you can't receive it by faith. A lot of people try to believe they are healed, but they have never started *hoping* they are healed. They don't have the image on the inside that they are healed, so their faith has nothing to motivate it and keep it on track.

One of the things you need to have, when it comes to fulfilling God's will and staying consistent over a long period of time, is a strong sense of hope. Hope is the anchor of your soul (Heb. 6:19). An anchor is what keeps a ship from being blown around. Hope will keep you from being blown off course and missing your destination. You need a vision—an image on the inside of you. Until you can see it on the inside, you won't see it on the outside.

A person who has seen a loved one die from sickness or mental disease can get an image of that illness burned into their mind. They can start to believe that illness runs in the family. It might not be a conscious thought, but they can see themselves dying from the same illness. They half expect it to happen, so it becomes a self-fulfilling prophecy because whatever image you have of yourself will eventually bear fruit (Prov. 23:7).

You need to see yourself as God sees you. His vision is revealed in the Word of God. Moses was 120 years old when he died, and his eyesight was not dim nor his natural force abated (Deut. 34:7). In this society, people talk about being "over the hill" at 40. They look at sick people in their 70s or 80s and think, *I'm going to be like that one day.* People start talking about and anticipating the problems they are going to have, and it becomes a self-fulfilling prophecy. You have a superior covenant to what Moses had, so if he could live 120 years and be healthy, you can too. You have to change the way you think. Study the Word and imagine the truths of God until it paints a picture on the inside of you—until you see yourself healthy, righteous, and full of peace and joy.

The Hebrew word *yetser* ("imagination") also means "conception" (*Strong's Concordance*). This reveals a significant truth: *Your imagination is where you conceive things.* This is really important. When a couple wants to have a baby, they can't just pray for one—they have to conceive the child. I have prayed for a lot of couples who were having trouble conceiving a baby. After I prayed for them to be healed, I always said, "This isn't going to be a virgin birth. You have a part to play in this situation. Faith without works is dead, so go and do your part." A baby has to be conceived through a physical relationship—you can't just pray for one. Similarly, your imagination is where you conceive a manifestation of God's miracle-working power. No imagination equals no conception.

Many people don't meditate on the Word of God until they conceive something. They throw out a prayer like "O God, heal me" or "Supply this need," but they haven't ever conceived from the Word what they are asking for. It's the equivalent of a married couple praying that a stork will bring them a baby. It isn't going to happen that way. First you have to conceive in your imagination what the Word says. For example, you have to see yourself healed.

The building that our ministry is currently in is 110,000 square feet, but when we bought the building, only 10,000 square feet was finished office space. The rest was an empty warehouse. After the architects drew up the plans and we were waiting for the funding to start on the construction, I had them place tape on the floor where all of the walls would be.

I spent hundreds of hours walking around inside the taped lines in that empty warehouse. I was *seeing* the walls in place and *picturing* how everything was going to look. I never stepped over the tape; I always entered where a door would be. Some people might think this is strange, but I was helping my imagination. I would look at the architect's drawings and then walk around inside the taped lines, *imagining* all the walls in place. I would see people inside the auditorium. In fact, I put a piece of plywood on top of several five-gallon buckets and stood on the platform and preached. No one was even in the building—it was nighttime and the warehouse was dark—but I preached like the auditorium was filled to capacity.

I used my imagination to see what I was believing God to do. On the day we held the dedication ceremony, after the building was completed, everyone was excited to see what God had done. A woman came up to me and said, "You don't look very excited. Aren't you delighted to have the building complete?" I was excited, but it was almost anticlimactic to see it with my eyes—because I had already seen it in my heart. For more than a year, I had seen on the inside what just then became visible to the physical eye. By the time construction was completed, I was ready to move on to the next task God had for me.

Today very few visionaries exist because life tries to beat this attitude out of us. Most kids are told by the adults around them to quit dreaming—to quit using their imaginations. Adults tend to think of visualizing the future as fantasizing, but there is a *big* difference between imagination and fantasy. "Imagination" is the power, or process, of seeing something you can't see with your physical eyes, whereas "fantasy" is delusion. Fantasy is imagining something that isn't real—it's fiction. I'm not talking about daydreaming; I'm talking about knowing the Word of God and seeing the spiritual truths it reveals. A sanctified, godly imagination is the part of us that conceives the things of God; it's the creative part of us that has a vision for the future.

Vision, in this sense, isn't seeing with your eyes; it's seeing with your heart. As a born-again believer filled with the Holy Spirit, you have the ability to see things that can't be seen with the natural eye. When I pray for people, I see them healed in my imagination. I see God touching their hearts. God will show me parts of a person's body that are injured or sick. I don't see it with my eyes—I get a mental picture.

Take the Word of God, and let it soak down into the creative part of your mind—your imagination—until you can see yourself successful or healed. Allow the Word to get down inside of you and generate vision until you see yourself laying hands on the sick and watching them recover—or see the business you want to start successful.

A godly imagination is directly tied to glorifying God and being thankful. The Bible says that if you don't glorify God and if you aren't thankful, your imagination becomes vain (Rom. 1:21). It's automatic. Instead of being creative and conceiving good things, a vain imagination conceives evil.

Some children are told from a young age that they aren't wanted or that they will never amount to anything. Other people in society are put down because of their skin color, lack of education, or socioeconomic status. When we believe the negative words or ideas that are pushed on us, it forms an image on the inside of us about who we are and what we can do. That image becomes a ceiling we can't rise above. Even though our talents and abilities could enable us to go further, we don't allow them to—somehow we find a way to self-destruct.

I have a very good friend whose father was pretty hard on him as a kid. They had a lot of cars on their property, and his father would make him help work on the cars. He told him, "You're so stupid, you can't screw a nut on a bolt without crossing the threads." Over the years, I have worked with my friend on a number of cars, and it seems like every time he puts a nut on a bolt, he cross-threads it. He would put it on once, and it would be okay. But then he would say, "I think I've cross-threaded it." So, he would take the nut off and put it back on five or six times, trying to get it right. Eventually, he would cross-thread the bolt. He had a negative image painted on the inside of him that still affects him.

A lot of people have been cursed in this way. You might not call it being "cursed," but that's what it is. Maybe you were cursed or you cursed yourself by being self-critical, or maybe you have done some really stupid things that have caused you to see yourself as a failure. All of these things will cause your imagination to become vain. You don't see yourself being who God says you are. God says you can lay hands on the sick and they shall recover (Mark 16:18), but you don't see it. You see yourself as a nobody, and religion reinforces the idea that you are an unworthy nobody. It teaches you to think, *Who am I to think God wants to do anything for me?* Then the experiences of life come along to strengthen all of the negative images you have formed about yourself.

Glorifying God, putting value and worth on Him, and being thankful will cause your imagination to come alive and start working for you. Instead of conceiving negative images, you'll start to conceive positive ideas. A positive imagination will help erase all of the self-defeating ideas you have wrongly believed about yourself, and you will begin to imagine yourself the way God sees you.

I had a chance to visit with Oral Roberts in 2009, and it made my imagination come alive. I don't agree with everything Oral Roberts did, but he had a heart for God; I can learn from him. We can't be so biased that we won't listen to anyone who doesn't agree with us 100 percent. Here's a news flash: *We don't have it all together either.* Nobody does. But we can still learn from one another. It's the same as if we are driving down the interstate and someone else is five hours down the road in front of us. It doesn't matter if they are the greatest person or have made all of the right decisions; they can still tell us what the road is like, where to eat, or where to buy gas.

I learned things from Oral. Hearing him tell about the things God had spoken to him inspired my imagination. Within a matter of months of speaking with Oral, God led me into the next major step for our ministry. Being around people who talk about vision causes you to dream big also. Most people think too small. They aim at nothing and hit it every time. It has become a cliché, but you need to aim for the moon; even if you miss, you might hit the stars.

When we were constructing the Charis Bible College facility in Colorado Springs, Colorado, we tried to get it finished by August so that we could start the school year in the new building. It wasn't finished until November, though, so it put us in a little bit of a bind. The old building was just way too small. One of the inconveniences was that we didn't have enough toilets, so the men had to use portable outdoor toilets—and Colorado can get cold in October.

When we finally moved into the new building, I had somebody ask me if it was a disappointment not to make the move by August. I said, "We raised $3.2 million above our normal expenses in fourteen months. I'd call that a smashing success." Being three months late was no big deal. I've never done anything perfectly in my life, so it didn't bother me. I still had a great miracle come in. We have to focus on the positive.

In order for your imagination to function positively, you need to spend time being quiet and still. Being busy with the things of this world and constantly watching television or listening to the radio will choke out your imagination. You have to spend some time being quiet and letting your imagination run wild. Be still and know that God is the Almighty. You might be amazed what things you conceive, and once you see it on the inside, you will see it on the outside.

II. Hope is your *imagination* (Rom. 8:24-25), and faith is the *substance* of things hoped for.

Now faith is the substance of things hoped for, the evidence of things not seen.
HEBREWS 11:1

A. If you can't hope for something first (i.e., imagine it), then you can't receive it by faith.

B. One of the things you need to have, when it comes to fulfilling God's will and staying consistent over a long period of time, is a strong sense of hope.

C. Hope is the anchor of your soul (Heb. 6:19).

   i.   Hope will keep you from being blown off course and missing your destination.

D. The Hebrew word *yetser* ("imagination") also means "conception" (*Strong's Concordance*)—this reveals a significant truth: *Your imagination is where you conceive things.*

E. You have to conceive in your imagination what the Word says; for example, you have to see yourself healed.

F. But there is a *big* difference between imagination and fantasy.

   i.   "Imagination" is the power, or process, of seeing something you can't see with your physical eyes, whereas "fantasy" is delusion.

   ii. Fantasy is imagining something that isn't real—it's fiction.

G. A sanctified, godly imagination is the part of you that conceives the things of God; it's the creative part of you that has a vision for the future.

H. Take the Word of God, and let it soak down into the creative part of your mind— your imagination—until you can see yourself successful or healed.

I. A godly imagination is directly tied to glorifying God and being thankful.

J. The Bible says that if you don't glorify God and if you aren't thankful, your imagination becomes vain (Rom. 1:21)—instead of being creative and conceiving good things, a vain imagination conceives evil.

K. When you believe negative words or ideas that are pushed on you, it forms an image on the inside of you about who you are and what you can do.

L. Even though your talents and abilities could enable you to go further, you don't allow them to—somehow you find a way to self-destruct.

M. You don't see yourself being who God says you are.

N. Glorifying God, putting value and worth on Him, and being thankful will cause your imagination to come alive and start working for you.

O. A positive imagination will help erase all of the self-defeating ideas you have wrongly believed about yourself, and you will begin to imagine yourself the way God sees you.

2. Hope is your *imagination* (Rom. 8:24-25), and faith is the *substance* of things hoped for.

> *Now faith is the substance of things hoped for, the evidence of things not seen.*
> HEBREWS 11:1

If you can't hope for something first (i.e., imagine it), then you can't receive it by faith. One of the things you need to have, when it comes to fulfilling God's will and staying consistent over a long period of time, is a strong sense of hope. Hope is the anchor of your soul (Heb. 6:19). Hope will keep you from being blown off course and missing your destination. The Hebrew word *yetser* ("imagination") also means "conception" (*Strong's Concordance*)—this reveals a significant truth: *Your imagination is where you conceive things*. You have to conceive in your imagination what the Word says; for example, you have to see yourself healed. But there is a *big* difference between imagination and fantasy. "Imagination" is the power, or process, of seeing something you can't see with your physical eyes, whereas "fantasy" is delusion. Fantasy is imagining something that isn't real—it's fiction. A sanctified, godly imagination is the part of you that conceives the things of God; it's the creative part of you that has a vision for the future. Take the Word of God, and let it soak down into the creative part of your mind—your imagination—until you can see yourself successful or healed. A godly imagination is directly tied to glorifying God and being thankful. The Bible says that if you don't glorify God and if you aren't thankful, your imagination becomes vain (Rom. 1:21)—instead of being creative and conceiving good things, a vain imagination conceives evil. When you believe negative words or ideas that are pushed on you, it forms an image on the inside of you about who you are and what you can do. Even though your talents and abilities could enable you to go further, you don't allow them to—somehow you find a way to self-destruct. You don't see yourself being who God says you are. Glorifying God, putting value and worth on Him, and being thankful will cause your imagination to come alive and start working for you. A positive imagination will help erase all of the self-defeating ideas you have wrongly believed about yourself, and you will begin to imagine yourself the way God sees you.

2a. _____ is your *imagination* (Rom. 8:24-25), and _____ is the *substance* of things hoped for (Heb. 11:1).
   A. Faith / hope
   B. Hope / Jesus
   C. Hope / faith
   D. All of the above
   E. None of the above
   C. Hope / faith

2b. Discussion question: What do you think about the statement, "If you can't hope for something first (i.e., imagine it), then you can't receive it by faith"?
   Discussion question

2c. What does Hebrews 6:19 tell you?
   That hope is the anchor of your soul

2d. Discussion question: How will hope keep you from being blown off course and missing your destination?
   Discussion question

2e. Is there a big difference between imagination and fantasy?
<u>Yes</u>

2f. Discussion question: How do they differ (see #2e)? In what ways have you seen either or both in your life?
<u>Discussion question</u>

2g. A positive imagination will help erase all of the _____ ideas you have _____ believed about yourself, and you will begin to imagine yourself the way _____ sees you.
<u>Self-defeating / wrongly / God</u>

7. _____ is your *imagination* (Rom. 8:24-25), and _____ is the *substance* of things hoped for (Heb. 11:1).
   A. Faith / hope
   B. Hope / Jesus
   C. Hope / faith
   D. All of the above
   E. None of the above

8. Discussion question: What do you think about the statement, "If you can't hope for something first (i.e., imagine it), then you can't receive it by faith"?

   _____

   _____

   _____

9. What does Hebrews 6:19 tell you?

   _____

   _____

   _____

10. Discussion question: How will hope keep you from being blown off course and missing your destination?

    _____

    _____

    _____

11. Is there a big difference between imagination and fantasy?

    _____

    _____

    _____

12. Discussion question: How do they differ (see #11)? In what ways have you seen either or both in your life?

_____

_____

_____

13. A positive imagination will help erase all of the _____ ideas you have _____ believed about yourself, and you will begin to imagine yourself the way _____ sees you.

7. C. Hope / faith
8. *Discussion question*
9. That hope is the anchor of your soul
10. *Discussion question*
11. Yes
12. *Discussion question*
13. Self-defeating / wrongly / God

HEBREWS 11:1
Now faith is the substance of things hoped for, the evidence of things not seen.

ROMANS 8:24-25
For we are saved by hope: but hope that is seen is not hope: for what a man seeth, why doth he yet hope for? [25] But if we hope for that we see not, then do we with patience wait for it.

HEBREWS 6:19
Which hope we have as an anchor of the soul, both sure and stedfast, and which entereth into that within the veil.

PROVERBS 23:7
For as he thinketh in his heart, so is he: Eat and drink, saith he to thee; but his heart is not with thee.

DEUTERONOMY 34:7
And Moses was an hundred and twenty years old when he died: his eye was not dim, nor his natural force abated.

ROMANS 1:21
Because that, when they knew God, they glorified him not as God, neither were thankful; but became vain in their imaginations, and their foolish heart was darkened.

MARK 16:18
They shall take up serpents; and if they drink any deadly thing, it shall not hurt them; they shall lay hands on the sick, and they shall recover.

LESSON 15.3

In the New Testament, the same word that was translated "imagination" was sometimes translated "understanding." The Bible is full of references to the importance of having understanding. In the Gospel of Matthew, Jesus taught that when people lack understanding, Satan will come and steal the Word that has been sown in their hearts (Matt. 13:19). Understanding is how we get something down on the inside of us. We have to let the truths of God go beyond mental awareness and down to the level of understanding where we can conceive a picture in our imagination.

Understanding is more than just knowledge or the ability to recall a fact. A lot of people read the Bible with their heads—not with their imaginations or hearts. That's like chewing food but not swallowing it. The Word won't minister to us at its fullest until we get it down to the level of understanding. It isn't enough to merely hear the things of God; we have to meditate on the Word until it paints a picture, until we truly see what is happening. That's how we use our imagination to conceive the things of God in our hearts.

I remember reading about David and Goliath when I was a kid. Scholars believed Goliath was nine feet nine inches tall, so I went outside and marked that height on a tree. Then I bent over until I was about five feet tall, which is how tall they thought David was. I wanted to get an image of what David was facing. You don't necessarily need to act out Bible stories, but you will get more out of the Word of God once you engage your imagination.

Eventually, I traveled to Israel on a tour. On a particularly hot day, we were on a bus that passed through the Valley of Elah where David fought Goliath. They asked if anybody wanted to get off the bus. It was so hot that I was the only one who wanted to leave the air conditioning. I got off the bus and walked down to a little streambed that ran through the valley. I picked up five small stones and stood there wondering what it must have been like for David to face Goliath with five little rocks. The reason people say that visiting Israel makes the Bible more real to them is because being "on location" engages their imagination. Once they see it, the Word comes alive.

Very few people meditate on the Word. Most simply read it in order to check off another good work on their list of religious duties, hoping it will obligate God to move in their lives. They read the Bible out of compulsion, so they run through it as fast as they can. After all, they wouldn't want to miss their favorite television show. At that level, they are just reading words and putting information in their brains. It never makes its way down into their hearts or imaginations, so they never conceive anything. It doesn't become alive to them.

Imagination isn't something we can afford to ignore. I've heard of a multi-millionaire entrepreneur who travels and speaks about business and wealth. Every week, he takes one day off just to be quiet and think. He doesn't conduct any business on that day; he just takes inventory of where he is and where he is going. Essentially, he is *fueling* his imagination. This is one of the practices that helped him succeed and earn millions of dollars.

We would be much better off if we spent time encouraging our imaginations. We can't allow other people to spoon-feed us all the time. We also have to ask God what *He* has for us. We can't let what other people say determine our identity and future. We need to find out what the Word says about us. Then we need to pray and let the Holy Spirit give us an image of what He wants us to do—and who He wants us to be. We can't become who God says we are until we can see ourselves as He sees us. Once we can see it on the inside, we can become it on the outside.

We will become exactly what we imagine—whether that image is positive or negative. If we think we are failures, we will be. We have to deal with our imagination and get it to line up with God's opinion of us.

Greater Things

I began believing it was possible to see people raised from the dead after reading what Jesus said in the Gospel of John:

> *Verily, verily, I say unto you, He that believeth on me, the works that I do shall he do also; and greater works than these shall he do; because I go unto my Father.*
> JOHN 14:12

I read that verse, and it inspired me to believe that God would do miracles through me. I thought about all of the miracles Jesus performed. I meditated on how He had called Lazarus out of his tomb, and asked, "Father, can I raise someone from the dead?" I meditated on it so much that I raised a dozen people from the dead every night in my dreams. I had dreams about going into morgues and emptying them out. After about six months, I actually saw a person raised from the dead with my physical eyes—but I had to see it with my heart *first*.

How you see yourself is important. You have to see yourself as able to do, or be, the things you are praying for. You won't see miracles come to pass if you don't believe that God can do a miracle through you. It needs to become so real in your imagination that you dream about it.

I saw two people raised from the dead, but then ten or fifteen years went by before I saw it again. One day, I remembered how I used to meditate on seeing people raised from the dead and decided that I needed to get my imagination going again in that area. I felt inspired by God to start imagining people being raised from the dead, so pretty soon, I was dreaming about it.

Then, one night, I got a phone call that my own son had died. He had been dead for four-and-a-half hours when I got the call. But I just started thanking God for His goodness and magnifying Him above the circumstances. By the time I arrived at the hospital, my son had come back to life—and it wouldn't have happened if I hadn't been meditating and imagining God's "raising-from-the-dead" power.

Before you see something happen, you have to be focused on it. It has to become so real that you see yourself doing it in your dreams. You won't see the miraculous power of God if you are defeated, discouraged, or depressed in your imagination. The Word says that as a man thinks in his heart, so is he (Prov. 23:7). You have to resurrect your imagination and start using it in a positive way.

Hope

I researched every time the word "imagination" was used in the Bible, and with the exception of one verse (1 Chr. 29:18), it was always used in a negative way. For instance, God saw that the imagination of man's heart was only evil continually (Gen. 6:5). At the tower of Babel, God said that nothing mankind could imagine would be restrained from them, so He divided language so that man wouldn't be united anymore (Gen. 11:6-7). (It's worth noting that God recognized the cumulative imagination of people could threaten His purpose for mankind. This shows how powerful imagination is.)

In the New Testament, it says,

(For the weapons of our warfare are not carnal, but mighty through God to the pulling down of strong holds;) **[5]** *Casting down imaginations, and every high thing that exalteth itself against the knowledge of God, and bringing into captivity every thought to the obedience of Christ.*

2 CORINTHIANS 10:4-5

Imagination is always referred to as negative. It used to puzzle me that imagination could be such a powerful thing but always carry negative connotations in Scripture. I prayed about it until the Lord showed me the answer:

For we are saved by hope: but hope that is seen is not hope: for what a man seeth, why doth he yet hope for? **[25]** *But if we hope for that we see not, then do we with patience wait for it.*

ROMANS 8:24-25

Hope, according to Scripture, is seeing something that you can't physically see. It's no longer hope if you can see it. *Hope is seeing something with your heart that you can't see with your eyes—which is exactly what imagination is.* It's the ability to see something that isn't present, the ability to see with your heart. I believe that hope is the scriptural word for a positive imagination. *Hope is your imagination working for you instead of against you.*

We need a strong sense of hope. *"Faith is the substance of things hoped for, the evidence of things not seen"* (Heb. 11:1). Faith only provides what hope has already seen. Hope is to faith what a thermostat is to an air conditioning system. *Hope* turns on the ability of God, while *faith* is the power that makes things come to pass.

I heard Charles Capps tell a story about a thermostat one time. It was probably made up, but the story illustrates a good point. He told about a man who was from the mountains but had never been around modern conveniences. He went to a meeting in the city. The meeting room he was in became hot as it filled with hundreds of people. The man was fanning himself to cool down, as he watched an usher walk by him and turn a dial on a small box that was mounted on the wall. Shortly thereafter, he started to feel cool air blowing on him. He was overwhelmed, so he went and asked the usher what he did to make the air cold.

"What do you mean?" the usher asked.

"You turned that little thing on the wall, and cold air started blowing," the man said.

"Well, yeah, it's a thermostat," the usher answered.

"Can I get one of those?" the man asked.

"Of course you can," he answered. "They sell them at any hardware store."

The man was excited and went straight to the hardware store to buy one. When he got back to his cabin in the mountains, he mounted the thermostat on the wall. He turned the dial and sat down to wait for the cold air. But, of course, nothing happened, because the thermostat has to be connected to an air conditioning system. A thermostat doesn't cool air—it activates the power unit that cools the air.

Likewise, faith only produces what hope has already seen. You have to have hope—or a positive imagination in your heart—that sees miracles happening. Just like a thermostat can be turned to hot or cold, your imagination can be negative or positive. Hope is a positive imagination. If your imagination is negative, you will see failure on the inside, leading you to experience failure on the outside. But if you are hoping and seeing a miracle in your heart, it will turn on the power of God to see that miracle manifest in your life.

Faith will either work *for* you or *against* you. A negative image will cause everything in you to work toward making the negative image you have bear fruit. You have to change the image that is inside of you by creating hope. Hope comes through the Word of God (Rom. 15:4). This is the first step of faith.

Notice that Romans 8:24-25 says we are saved by hope because we wait with patience for what we do not see. Earlier, I taught how important patience is in fulfilling God's will for our lives. I also shared that patience is simply faith over a prolonged period of time. Patience is also linked to hope and your imagination. If you have a strong sense of hope, or a strong imagination, then you will have the patience to wait for God's will to manifest in your life—even if it takes a long time.

A strong sense of hope will cause you to know beyond the shadow of a doubt that God's will is going to come to pass. You will know it in your heart and expect it because your imagination has made it real. No matter what might be going on in your life, you will know that you have what you are waiting for.

Our *Healing Journeys 2* DVD tells the story of a woman named Merci Santos who was healed of multiple sclerosis. One of the things she said—when she was in a wheelchair and everyone told her that she would never walk again—was she just knew it wasn't true. She saw herself healed and knew that one day, she would be. She needed someone to teach her some things and activate her faith, but she saw herself well despite the fact that her symptoms were getting worse and worse. That is what hope is. Hope won't get you healed, but it will provide the motivation for your faith to get you healed.

Sometimes you just need to be real with yourself and say, "I may not be in a place right now where I can really believe that I'm going to be healed instantly, but I'm in the process of hoping. I'm building my hope, and I'm beginning to paint an image on the inside that I will be healed."

I met a man who had been diagnosed with bone cancer. He believed that he would be healed, and he was, but during the process, doctors surgically removed a part of his pubic bone. He wanted to use his faith to believe that his pubic bone would grow back. That's pretty strong faith—to grow something back that was cut out. Anyway, he cut out pictures of a human skeleton from an encyclopedia and put the pictures up in his house. He started to imagine his pubic bone growing back, and in a short period of time, it did. *He saw it on the inside, and it came to pass on the outside!*

We are living at such a substandard level in comparison to what God intends for us. *Most of us don't have a clue about the extent of the power God has placed inside every born-again believer.* I can show scriptures that say we have the same power inside of us that raised Christ from the dead. But it doesn't matter whether we can quote Scripture—we have to believe it.

Can you see yourself raising the dead? Have you seen yourself standing against the devil and overcoming illness or poverty? Can you see yourself doing the miracles Jesus did? You have to meditate on the Word of God until you can see yourself doing these things. You have to get your imagination working. The reason the Word says that hope is so powerful is because once you can see a manifestation of God's power with your heart, you can see it materialize in your life.

Andrew's Recommendations for Further Study:

If you want to know more about Merci Santos' testimony, I encourage you to order the *Healing Journeys, Volume 2* DVD.

III. In the New Testament, the same word that was translated "imagination" was sometimes translated "understanding."

    A. The Bible is full of references to the importance of having understanding (Matt. 13:19).

    B. Understanding is how we get something down on the inside of us.

    C. The Word won't minister to us at its fullest until we get it down to the level of understanding.

    D. We have to meditate on the Word until it paints a picture, until we truly see what is happening.

    E. That's how we use our imagination to conceive the things of God in our hearts.

    F. We will get more out of the Word of God once we engage our imaginations.

    G. We would be much better off if we spent time encouraging our imaginations—we can't allow other people to spoon-feed us all the time.

    H. We also can't let what other people say determine our identity and future.

    I. We need to find out what the Word says about us; then we need to pray and let the Holy Spirit give us an image of what He wants us to do—and who He wants us to be.

        i. We can't become who God says we are until we can see ourselves as He sees us.

    J. We will become exactly what we imagine—whether that image is positive or negative.

IV. How you see yourself is important.

    A. You have to see yourself as able to do, or be, the things you are praying for.

    B. You won't see miracles come to pass if you don't believe that God can do a miracle through you.

    C. Before you see something happen, you have to be focused on it.

    D. It has to become so real that you see yourself doing it in your dreams.

    E. You won't see the miraculous power of God if you are defeated, discouraged, or depressed in your imagination.

    F. The Word says that as a man thinks in his heart, so is he (Prov. 23:7).

    G. You have to resurrect your imagination and start using it in a positive way.

V. I researched every time the word "imagination" was used in the Bible, and with the exception of one verse (1 Chr. 29:18), it was always used in a negative way.

A. It used to puzzle me that imagination could be such a powerful thing but always carry negative connotations in Scripture.

B. I prayed about it until the Lord showed me the answer:

For we are saved by hope: but hope that is seen is not hope: for what a man seeth, why doth he yet hope for? [25] But if we hope for that we see not, then do we with patience wait for it.

ROMANS 8:24-25

C. *Hope is seeing something with your heart that you can't see with your eyes—which is exactly what imagination is.*

D. I believe that hope is the scriptural word for a positive imagination.

E. *Hope is your imagination working for you instead of against you.*

F. Faith only provides what hope has already seen: *"Faith is the substance of things hoped for, the evidence of things not seen"* (Heb. 11:1).

G. *Hope* turns on the ability of God, while *faith* is the power that makes things come to pass.

H. Faith will either work *for* you or *against* you.

I. A negative image will cause everything in you to work toward making the negative image you have bear fruit.

J. You have to change the image that is inside of you by creating hope.

K. Hope comes through the Word of God (Rom. 15:4)—this is the first step of faith.

L. Notice that Romans 8:24-25 says you are saved by hope because you wait with patience for what you do not see—patience is also linked to hope and your imagination.

M. If you have a strong sense of hope, or a strong imagination, then you will have the patience to wait for God's will to manifest in your life—even if it takes a long time.

    i. A strong sense of hope will cause you to know beyond the shadow of a doubt that God's will is going to come to pass.

    ii. You will know it in your heart and expect it because your imagination has made it real.

    iii. No matter what might be going on in your life, you will know that you have what you are waiting for.

Andrew's Recommendations for Further Study:

If you want to know more about Merci Santos' testimony, I encourage you to order the Healing Journeys, Vol. 2 DVD.

3. In the New Testament, the same word that was translated "imagination" was sometimes translated "understanding." The Bible is full of references to the importance of having understanding (Matt. 13:19). Understanding is how we get something down on the inside of us. The Word won't minister to us at its fullest until we get it down to the level of understanding. We have to meditate on the Word until it paints a picture, until we truly see what is happening. That's how we use our imagination to conceive the things of God in our hearts. We will get more out of the Word of God once we engage our imaginations. We would be much better off if we spent time encouraging our imaginations—we can't allow other people to spoon-feed us all the time. We also can't let what other people say determine our identity and future. We need to find out what the Word says about us; then we need to pray and let the Holy Spirit give us an image of what He wants us to do—and who He wants us to be. We can't become who God says we are until we can see ourselves as He sees us. We will become exactly what we imagine—whether that image is positive or negative.

3a. In the New Testament, the same word that was translated "imagination" was sometimes translated _____.
A. "Understanding"
B. "Fantasy"
C. "Knowledge"
D. All of the above
E. None of the above
A. Understanding

3b. Understanding is how you what?
Get something down on the inside of you

3c. Discussion question: Why do you think that understanding makes a difference when reading and meditating on the Word?
Discussion question

3d. Discussion question: Take a scripture or a passage of Scripture and meditate on it using your imagination. In what ways, if any, does this change your perspective on this passage?
Discussion question

3e. True or false: You can't let what other people say determine your identity and future.
True

3f. You will become _____ what you imagine—whether that image is _____ or _____.
Exactly / positive / negative

4. How you see yourself is important. You have to see yourself as able to do, or be, the things you are praying for. You won't see miracles come to pass if you don't believe that God can do a miracle through you. Before you see something happen, you have to be focused on it. It has to become so real that you see yourself doing it in your dreams. You won't see the miraculous power of God if you are defeated, discouraged, or depressed in your imagination. The Word says that as a man thinks in his heart, so is he (Prov. 23:7). You have to resurrect your imagination and start using it in a positive way.

4a. How do you have to see yourself?
As able to do, or be, the things you are praying for

4b. Will you see miracles come to pass if you don't believe that God can do a miracle through you?
No

4c. Discussion question: To see something happen, you have to be focused on it, to the point where you see yourself doing it in your dreams. Have you ever been that focused on a goal or desire? If yes, what were the results of that? If no, what goals or desires do you believe you should be that focused on?
Discussion question

5. I researched every time the word "imagination" was used in the Bible, and with the exception of one verse (1 Chr. 29:18), it was always used in a negative way. It used to puzzle me that imagination could be such a powerful thing but always carry negative connotations in Scripture. I prayed about it until the Lord showed me the answer:

> *For we are saved by hope: but hope that is seen is not hope: for what a man seeth, why doth he yet hope for? [25] But if we hope for that we see not, then do we with patience wait for it.*

ROMANS 8:24-25

Hope is seeing something with your heart that you can't see with your eyes—which is exactly what imagination is. I believe that hope is the scriptural word for a positive imagination. Hope is your imagination working for you instead of against you. Faith only provides what hope has already seen: *"Faith is the substance of things hoped for, the evidence of things not seen"* (Heb. 11:1). *Hope* turns on the ability of God, while *faith* is the power that makes things come to pass. Faith will either work *for* you or *against* you. A negative image will cause everything in you to work toward making the negative image you have bear fruit. You have to change the image that is inside of you by creating hope. Hope comes through the Word of God (Rom. 15:4)—this is the first step of faith. Notice that Romans 8:24-25 says you are saved by hope because you wait with patience for what you do not see—patience is also linked to hope and your imagination. If you have a strong sense of hope, or a strong imagination, then you will have the patience to wait for God's will to manifest in your life—even if it takes a long time. A strong sense of hope will cause you to know beyond the shadow of a doubt that God's will is going to come to pass. You will know it in your heart and expect it because your imagination has made it real. No matter what might be going on in your life, you will know that you have what you are waiting for.

5a. According to Romans 8:24-25, what is hope?
Seeing something with your heart that you can't see with your eyes, exactly what imagination is

5b. Hebrews 11:1 says, *"Faith is the _____ of things _____ for, the evidence of things not seen."*
"Substance" / "hoped"

5c. Discussion question: In your life, how have you experienced the concept that hope turns on the ability of God, while faith is the power that makes things come to pass?
Discussion question

5d. What does Romans 15:4 say?
That hope comes through the Word of God

5e. Discussion question: How does having a strong sense of hope, or a strong imagination, give you the patience to wait for God's will to manifest in your life?
Discussion question

14. In the New Testament, the same word that was translated "imagination" was sometimes translated _____.
    A. "Understanding"
    B. "Fantasy"
    C. "Knowledge"
    D. All of the above
    E. None of the above

15. Understanding is how you what?

    _____

    _____

    _____

16. Discussion question: Why do you think that understanding makes a difference when reading and meditating on the Word?

    _____

    _____

    _____

17. Discussion question: Take a scripture or a passage of Scripture and meditate on it using your imagination. In what ways, if any, does this change your perspective on this passage?

    _____

    _____

    _____

18. True or false: You can't let what other people say determine your identity and future.

19. You will become _____ what you imagine—whether that image is _____ or _____.

20. How do you have to see yourself?

    _____

    _____

    _____

21. Will you see miracles come to pass if you don't believe that God can do a miracle through you?

_____

_____

_____

22. Discussion question: To see something happen, you have to be focused on it, to the point where you see yourself doing it in your dreams. Have you ever been that focused on a goal or desire? If yes, what were the results of that? If no, what goals or desires do you believe you should be that focused on?

_____

_____

_____

23. According to Romans 8:24-25, what is hope?

_____

_____

_____

24. Hebrews 11:1 says, _"Faith is the _____ of things _____ for, the evidence of things not seen."_

25. Discussion question: In your life, how have you experienced the concept that hope turns on the ability of God, while faith is the power that makes things come to pass?

_____

_____

_____

26. What does Romans 15:4 say?

_____

_____

_____

27. Discussion question: How does having a strong sense of hope, or a strong imagination, give you the patience to wait for God's will to manifest in your life?

_____

_____

_____

14. A. "Understanding"
15. Get something down on the inside of you
16. *Discussion question*
17. *Discussion question*
18. True
19. Exactly / positive / negative
20. As able to do, or be, the things you are praying for
21. No
22. *Discussion question*
23. Seeing something with your heart that you can't see with your eyes, exactly what imagination is
24. *"Substance" / "hoped"*
25. *Discussion question*
26. That hope comes through the Word of God
27. *Discussion question*

MATTHEW 13:19
When any one heareth the word of the kingdom, and understandeth it not, then cometh the wicked one, and catcheth away that which was sown in his heart. This is he which received seed by the way side.

JOHN 14:12
Verily, verily, I say unto you, He that believeth on me, the works that I do shall he do also; and greater works than these shall he do; because I go unto my Father.

PROVERBS 23:7
For as he thinketh in his heart, so is he: Eat and drink, saith he to thee; but his heart is not with thee.

1 CHRONICLES 29:18
O Lord God of Abraham, Isaac, and of Israel, our fathers, keep this for ever in the imagination of the thoughts of the heart of thy people, and prepare their heart unto thee.

GENESIS 6:5
And God saw that the wickedness of man was great in the earth, and that every imagination of the thoughts of his heart was only evil continually.

GENESIS 11:6-7
And the Lord said, Behold, the people is one, and they have all one language; and this they begin to do: and now nothing will be restrained from them, which they have imagined to do. [7] Go to, let us go down, and there confound their language, that they may not understand one another's speech.

2 CORINTHIANS 10:4-5
(For the weapons of our warfare are not carnal, but mighty through God to the pulling down of strong holds;) [5] Casting down imaginations, and every high thing that exalteth itself against the knowledge of God, and bringing into captivity every thought to the obedience of Christ.

ROMANS 8:24-25
For we are saved by hope: but hope that is seen is not hope: for what a man seeth, why doth he yet hope for? [25] But if we hope for that we see not, then do we with patience wait for it.

HEBREWS 11:1
Now faith is the substance of things hoped for, the evidence of things not seen.

ROMANS 15:4
For whatsoever things were written aforetime were written for our learning, that we through patience and comfort of the scriptures might have hope.

LESSON 15.4

A positive imagination is a byproduct of you being truly thankful and valuing the things of God (Rom. 1:21). Prizing God and being thankful will cause your imagination to come alive, and you will start seeing things differently than you have ever seen them before. But if you don't magnify God and remain thankful, your imagination will become negative, and then your heart becomes hardened. The scripture we have been studying says that they *"became vain in their imaginations, and their foolish heart was darkened"* (Rom. 1:21). A foolish, darkened heart is a hardened heart—and once your heart is hardened, you are separated from the life of God (Eph. 4:18).

It's tragic, but most people live somewhere between a vain, negative imagination and a hardened heart. They only imagine bad things, so when the doctor tells them they are going to die, they start planning their funerals. They see themselves dying and start to imagine what is going to happen when they are gone. Such a vain, negative imagination works against them and causes a hardened heart. Having a hard heart doesn't necessarily mean you aren't trying to love God or follow His will for your life; it means you don't understand how much God loves you—He loves you totally separate from your behavior or performance.

People with hardened hearts only see and understand the Word of God with their brains. Moving beyond that stage takes time and effort. You have to start obeying God, meditating on the Word, glorifying the Lord, and being thankful. As you focus more on God, your imagination will come alive, and you will have a strong sense of hope about your future and the things God has promised you. Those practices will keep you focused on God and what He has already done for you, instead of being focused on yourself. It will help you stay on track to fulfill God's will for your life.

You need to have a vision that you are moving toward. Vision is nothing but hope for the future—or a positive imagination. It will give you the motivation to keep going and the focus to fulfill God's will for your life. The Apostle Paul wrote,

While we look not at the things which are seen, but at the things which are not seen: for the things which are seen are temporal; but the things which are not seen are eternal.

2 CORINTHIANS 4:18

How was Paul looking at things that can't be seen? He was seeing them with his heart, or imagination. I was at a Charis Bible College meeting in Colorado one time when my wife was singing "Hallelujah" and everyone was worshiping God. The presence of the Lord was powerful. I was standing there with my eyes closed, and all of a sudden, I saw a picture in my mind of Jesus walking in through a set of double doors to my left. He walked through the doors and stood there as the doors slowly closed behind Him. He waited there for a moment, looking around. Then He walked up to a woman on the front row, touched her, and she fell to the floor, worshiping and praising God. Then He walked past two people and touched another woman. When Jesus touched her, she went down on her knees, lifted up her hands, and started worshiping God. My eyes were closed the whole time—I was seeing it happen in my imagination.

What I was seeing in my imagination was so real that I opened my physical eyes to see if it was really happening. When I opened my eyes, the two doors on my left flew open. I couldn't see anyone standing there, but the doors burst open and then slowly closed. Just after the doors closed, the woman I had seen Jesus touch fell flat on the floor. A moment later, the second woman hit her knees and started praising God. Everything I saw in my imagination happened. I saw it with my physical eyes, except I couldn't see Jesus. All I could see with my eyes were the physical things that were happening. I couldn't see what was happening in the spiritual realm.

I could actually see better with my heart than I could with my eyes, so I closed my eyes again. In my imagination, I saw Jesus stand beside me and minister to me. Then I saw Him walk down the center aisle of the room and touch some other people. I kept my eyes closed and watched it all play out in my imagination—I could see it better on the inside than I could with my physical eyes. After the service was over, I went up to the people I saw Jesus touch in my imagination and asked if they experienced anything during the service. They told me what had happened to them, and it was exactly what I had seen in my heart.

God created you to be so much more than most of you are experiencing. Most of you are going through this life half-blind, only seeing with your natural eyes. If you try to run a race half-blind, you are probably going to trip over something. Likewise, you can't fulfill God's will for your life without using your heart to see.

Getting into the presence of God will allow you to see things in your imagination. Everything in the physical might be indicating one thing, but in your heart, the Word of God can paint a picture of something else. The natural evidence might suggest that your business is going to fail, but you could have an image on the inside and know beyond the shadow of a doubt that it will succeed. Conceive the miracle in your imagination—then watch it come to pass.

None are blinder than a group of people who direct their lives by what they can only physically see, sense, or understand. Faith is the ability to see things that aren't physically present. You must have a vision to fulfill God's will for your life. Proverbs says that *"where there is no vision, the people perish"* (Prov. 29:18). Many people are falling by the wayside simply because they lack vision. They don't have any direction, so they are stumbling through life, bouncing from one problem to the next like a pinball. You can't allow circumstances to dictate your direction like that.

Find the purpose God has for you. Seek the Lord and learn to hear His voice. Then set a goal, and do something constructive with your life. Live your life so that when you are gone, people are going to miss you. You will have to leave the safety and security the world offers and take some chances, but that's why God sent the Holy Spirit to help you. Fruit grows out on the limb; you can't be a trunk-hugger and bear fruit. You have to get out on the limb, where you're blowing in the wind and hanging on for dear life.

Glorify God and recognize what He has done in your life. Remember that if worse comes to worst, you are going to heaven for all eternity. Be thankful and magnify God above your circumstances. Take control and begin to conceive the purposes of God in your imagination. Let the plan God has for you take root in your heart, see yourself fulfilling it, and then watch as it comes to pass.

You won't fulfill God's plan for your life overnight; you have to be patient. It may take God some time to get you back on track and heading in the right direction, but if you make seeking God your lifestyle, things will start to happen. In a short period of time, your imagination will come alive. Your heart won't be darkened anymore. Instead, you will begin to hear and see things that you couldn't hear or see before. God will start directing you—putting you on track to fulfill His purpose for your life.

Father, I pray that the truths in this study guide have helped people to find, follow, and ultimately fulfill Your perfect will for their lives. Bring back to their remembrance the things You have spoken to them through these teachings and give them the wisdom to apply their lives to them. Thank You, Jesus, for the awesome things that are in store for each one of them. Amen!

VI. A positive imagination is a byproduct of you being truly thankful and valuing the things of God (Rom. 1:21).

   A. But if you don't magnify God and remain thankful, your imagination will become negative, and then your heart becomes hardened.

   B. A foolish, darkened heart (Rom. 1:21) is a hardened heart—and once your heart is hardened, you are separated from the life of God (Eph. 4:18).

   C. Having a hard heart doesn't necessarily mean you aren't trying to love God or follow His will for your life; it means you don't understand how much God loves you— He loves you totally separate from your behavior or performance.

   D. Moving beyond that stage takes time and effort: You have to start obeying God, meditating on the Word, glorifying the Lord, and being thankful.

   E. You need to have a vision that you are moving toward.

      i. Vision is nothing but hope for the future—or a positive imagination.

   F. It will give you the motivation to keep going and the focus to fulfill God's will for your life.

   G. The Apostle Paul wrote,

     While we look not at the things which are seen, but at the things which are not seen: for the things which are seen are temporal; but the things which are not seen are eternal.

                            2 CORINTHIANS 4:18

   H. Paul was looking at things that can't be seen by seeing them with his heart, or imagination.

   I. You can't fulfill God's will for your life without using your heart to see.

   J. Everything in the physical might be indicating one thing, but in your heart, the Word of God can paint a picture of something else.

   K. Proverbs says that *"where there is no vision, the people perish"* (Prov. 29:18)—many people are falling by the wayside simply because they lack vision.

      i. They don't have any direction, so they are stumbling through life, bouncing from one problem to the next like a pinball.

      ii. You can't allow circumstances to dictate your direction like that.

      iii. Find the purpose God has for you.

   L. You won't fulfill God's plan for your life overnight; you have to be patient.

M. It may take God some time to get you back on track and heading in the right direction, but if you make seeking God your lifestyle, things will start to happen.

N. In a short period of time, your imagination will come alive; your heart won't be darkened anymore.

O. God will start directing you—putting you on track to fulfill His purpose for your life.

Father, I pray that the truths in this study guide have helped people to find, follow, and ultimately fulfill Your perfect will for their lives. Bring back to their remembrance the things You have spoken to them through these teachings and give them the wisdom to apply their lives to them. Thank You, Jesus, for the awesome things that are in store for each one of them. Amen!

6. A positive imagination is a byproduct of you being truly thankful and valuing the things of God (Rom. 1:21). But if you don't magnify God and remain thankful, your imagination will become negative, and then your heart becomes hardened. A foolish, darkened heart (Rom. 1:21) is a hardened heart—and once your heart is hardened, you are separated from the life of God (Eph. 4:18). Having a hard heart doesn't necessarily mean you aren't trying to love God or follow His will for your life; it means you don't understand how much God loves you—He loves you totally separate from your behavior or performance. Moving beyond that stage takes time and effort: You have to start obeying God, meditating on the Word, glorifying the Lord, and being thankful. You need to have a vision that you are moving toward. Vision is nothing but hope for the future—or a positive imagination. It will give you the motivation to keep going and the focus to fulfill God's will for your life. The Apostle Paul wrote,

> *While we look not at the things which are seen, but at the things which are not seen: for the things which are seen are temporal; but the things which are not seen are eternal.*

> 2 CORINTHIANS 4:18

Paul was looking at things that can't be seen by seeing them with his heart, or imagination. You can't fulfill God's will for your life without using your heart to see. Everything in the physical might be indicating one thing, but in your heart, the Word of God can paint a picture of something else. Proverbs says that *"where there is no vision, the people perish"* (Prov. 29:18)—many people are falling by the wayside simply because they lack vision. They don't have any direction, so they are stumbling through life, bouncing from one problem to the next like a pinball. You can't allow circumstances to dictate your direction like that. Find the purpose God has for you. You won't fulfill God's plan for your life overnight; you have to be patient. It may take God some time to get you back on track and heading in the right direction, but if you make seeking God your lifestyle, things will start to happen. In a short period of time, your imagination will come alive; your heart won't be darkened anymore. God will start directing you—putting you on track to fulfill His purpose for your life.

6a.　What is a positive imagination a byproduct of?
　　You being truly thankful and valuing the things of God (Rom. 1:21)

6b.　What does having a hardened heart *not* mean and what *does* it mean?
　　It doesn't necessarily mean you aren't trying to love God or follow His will for your life, and it does mean you don't understand how much God loves you—He love you totally separate from your behavior or performance

6c.　Discussion question: What is your vision (hope for the future, or positive imagination). If you do not have one, meditate on what you think your vision could or should be.
　　Discussion question

6d.   In 2 Corinthians 4:18, the Apostle Paul wrote, *"While we look not at the things which are seen, but at the things _____: for the things which are seen are temporal; but the things _____ are eternal."*
A.   *"Which are seen"*
B.   *"Which God hath spoken"*
C.   *"Which ye have prayed for"*
D.   All of the above
E.   None of the above
E.   None of the above

6e.   True or false: You can't fulfill God's will for your life without using your heart to see.
True

6f.   Discussion question: Have you ever faced a situation where everything in the physical was indicating one thing, but in your heart, the Word of God had painted a different picture? Share your experience.
Discussion question

6g.   You can't allow _____ to dictate your _____.
Circumstances / direction

Father, I pray that the truths in this study guide have helped people to find, follow, and ultimately fulfill Your perfect will for their lives. Bring back to their remembrance the things You have spoken to them through these teachings and give them the wisdom to apply their lives to them. Thank You, Jesus, for the awesome things that are in store for each one of them. Amen!

28.   What is a positive imagination a byproduct of?

_____

_____

_____

29.   What does having a hardened heart *not* mean and what *does* it mean?

_____

_____

_____

30.   Discussion question: What is your vision (hope for the future, or positive imagination). If you do not have one, meditate on what you think your vision could or should be.

_____

_____

_____

31.   In 2 Corinthians 4:18, the Apostle Paul wrote, "*While we look not at the things which are seen, but at the things _____: for the things which are seen are temporal; but the things _____ are eternal.*"
    A. "*Which are seen*"
    B. "*Which God hath spoken*"
    C. "*Which ye have prayed for*"
    D. All of the above
    E. None of the above

32.   True or false: You can't fulfill God's will for your life without using your heart to see.

33.   Discussion question: Have you ever faced a situation where everything in the physical was indicating one thing, but in your heart, the Word of God had painted a different picture? Share your experience.

_____

_____

_____

34.   You can't allow _____ to dictate your _____.

28. You being truly thankful and valuing the things of God (Rom. 1:21)
29. It doesn't necessarily mean you aren't trying to love God or follow His will for your life, and it does mean you don't understand how much God loves you—He love you totally separate from your behavior or performance
30. *Discussion question*
31. E.   None of the above
32. True
33. *Discussion question*
34. Circumstances / direction

ROMANS 1:21
Because that, when they knew God, they glorified him not as God, neither were thankful; but became vain in their imaginations, and their foolish heart was darkened.

EPHESIANS 4:18
Having the understanding darkened, being alienated from the life of God through the ignorance that is in them, because of the blindness of their heart.

2 CORINTHIANS 4:18
While we look not at the things which are seen, but at the things which are not seen: for the things which are seen are temporal; but the things which are not seen are eternal.

PROVERBS 29:18
Where there is no vision, the people perish: but he that keepeth the law, happy is he.

ANDREW'S TEACHING RECOMMENDATIONS IN THIS STUDY GUIDE

LESSON 11.1
Living in the Balance of Grace and Faith
Emphasize grace or faith to the exclusion of the other, and the imbalance will make it difficult to receive from God. If you have been struggling with confusion, frustration, and disappointment in your relationship with God, this teaching is for you.

Item Code: 1064-C   5-CD album
Item Code: 1064-D   As-Seen-on-TV DVD album
Item Code: 3208-D   Recorded Live DVD album
Item Code: 328   Paperback
Item Code: 428   Study Guide

LESSON 15.3
Healing Journeys, Vol. 2
Recorded here are five stories of the power of God's Word working in the lives of ordinary people. They all came to understand what God has already done for them through Jesus. Their stories will touch your heart and build your faith.

Item Code: 3008-D   Single DVD

OTHER RECOMMENDED TEACHINGS

Christian Survival Kit
Jesus knew His disciples would face the most trying time of their lives when He went to the cross. So, He gave them vital survival instructions that apply to your life today!

Item Code: 1001-C   16-CD album

Discover the Keys to Staying Full of God
Staying full of God is not a secret or a mystery; it's simple. For that reason, few people recognize the keys, and even fewer practice them. Learn what they are, and put them into practice. They will keep your heart sensitive.

Item Code: 1029-C   4-CD album
Item Code: 1029-D   As-Seen-on-TV DVD album
Item Code: 324   Paperback
Item Code: 424   Study Guide

Don't Limit God X 10
You are the one who determines who God is and what He can do in your life. He is waiting on you. If you doubt that now, you won't after listening to this message.

Item Code: 1076-C   5-CD album
Item Code: 1076-D   As-Seen-on-TV DVD album
Item Code: 3219-D   Recorded Live DVD album

Effortless Change
We all have areas in our lives we want to change. Trying to change from the outside in is difficult. Inside out is effortless. Learn why.

Item Code: 1018-C   4-CD album
Item Code: 1018-D   As-Seen-on-TV DVD album
Item Code: 331   Paperback
Item Code: 431   Study Guide

God's Man, Plan, and Timing
Moses was God's man, and he knew God's plan, but he didn't have a clue as to the timing or how to see the plan come to pass. This message from Andrew will reveal truths from the Moses' life that will ensure you don't make the same mistakes!

Item Code: U05-C   Single CD

OTHER RECOMMENDED TEACHINGS

Hardness of Heart
You might be surprised to find out that all Christians have a degree of hardness in their hearts. Listen as Andrew establishes from Scripture the cause and the cure.

Item Code: 1003-C   4-CD album
Item Code: 1003-D   As-Seen-on-TV DVD album
Item Code: 303   Paperback

Lessons from Elijah
You don't have to experience everything to learn life's lessons. Elijah, a man mightily used of God, is a great example. You'll be blessed from these life examples.

Item Code: 1026-C   5-CD album
Item Code: 1026-D   As-Seen-on-TV DVD album

The Power of Hope
Imagination dictates how your life goes, and if you're ever going to receive what God has for you, you'll need to understand that hope is a *positive* imagination. Learn this and you'll know the true power of hope!

Item Code: 1080-C   5-CD album
Item Code: 1080-D   As-Seen-on-TV DVD album
Item Code: 3221-D   Recorded Live DVD album